Cambridge Elements

Elements in Pragmatics
edited by
Jonathan Culpeper
Lancaster University, UK
Michael Haugh
University of Queensland, Australia

SPEECH ACT THEORY

Between Narrow and Broad Pragmatics

Stavros Assimakopoulos
University of Malta

CAMBRIDGE
UNIVERSITY PRESS

Shaftesbury Road, Cambridge CB2 8EA, United Kingdom

One Liberty Plaza, 20th Floor, New York, NY 10006, USA

477 Williamstown Road, Port Melbourne, VIC 3207, Australia

314–321, 3rd Floor, Plot 3, Splendor Forum, Jasola District Centre,
New Delhi – 110025, India

103 Penang Road, #05–06/07, Visioncrest Commercial, Singapore 238467

Cambridge University Press is part of Cambridge University Press & Assessment,
a department of the University of Cambridge.

We share the University's mission to contribute to society through the pursuit of
education, learning and research at the highest international levels of excellence.

www.cambridge.org
Information on this title: www.cambridge.org/9781009539357

DOI: 10.1017/9781009378376

© Stavros Assimakopoulos 2025

This publication is in copyright. Subject to statutory exception and to the provisions
of relevant collective licensing agreements, no reproduction of any part may take
place without the written permission of Cambridge University Press & Assessment.

When citing this work, please include a reference to the DOI 10.1017/9781009378376

First published 2025

A catalogue record for this publication is available from the British Library

ISBN 978-1-009-53935-7 Hardback
ISBN 978-1-009-37836-9 Paperback
ISSN 2633-6464 (online)
ISSN 2633-6456 (print)

Cambridge University Press & Assessment has no responsibility for the persistence
or accuracy of URLs for external or third-party internet websites referred to in this
publication and does not guarantee that any content on such websites is, or will remain,
accurate or appropriate.

For EU product safety concerns, contact us at Calle de José Abascal, 56, 1°, 28003
Madrid, Spain, or email eugpsr@cambridge.org

Speech Act Theory

Between Narrow and Broad Pragmatics

Elements in Pragmatics

DOI: 10.1017/9781009378376
First published online: December 2025

Stavros Assimakopoulos
University of Malta

Author for correspondence: Stavros Assimakopoulos, stavros.assimakopoulos@um.edu.mt

> **Abstract:** Speech act theory has been foundational in establishing pragmatics as an independent field of inquiry; yet, recent pragmatic research appears to have drifted away from the theoretical investigation of speech acts. This Element explores the reasons why this is so, focusing on the difference of perspective that emerges when the scope of the discipline is viewed through a narrow versus a broad lens. Following an overview of the initial exposition of speech act theory by Austin, it tracks its evolution, through subsequent Searlean and Gricean elaborations, to the currently received view. This view is then found to have diverged substantially from Austin's original vision, largely due to its alignment with the narrow conception of pragmatics. Against this backdrop, it is suggested that embracing the broad take on the discipline can allow for a reintegration of Austin's vision into the way we theorise about speech acts.

Keywords: speech acts, force, meaning, component/narrow pragmatics, perspective/broad pragmatics

© Stavros Assimakopoulos 2025

ISBNs: 9781009539357 (HB), 9781009378369 (PB), 9781009378376 (OC)
ISSNs: 2633-6464 (online), 2633-6456 (print)

Contents

1 Introduction — 1

2 Two Takes on the Scope of Pragmatics — 3

3 Speech Act Theory: Setting the Scene — 10

4 The Inception of Speech Act Theory — 11

5 The Received View of Speech Act Theory in Pragmatics — 25

6 Back to the Origins: An Evaluation of the Received View — 42

7 Speech Acts as Context-Driven Actions — 52

8 By Way of Conclusion — 62

References — 64

1 Introduction

The observation that language use quintessentially underlies the performance of actions, such as apologising, threatening, asserting, requesting, and so on, is neither controversial nor particularly ground-breaking in its own right. Even so, it has attracted an enormous amount of attention among scholars working not only in linguistics, philosophy, and cognitive science, but also in such diverse fields as literary criticism, social science, argumentation theory, artificial intelligence, and law studies. The main reason for this does not, of course, lie with the fact that people are capable of performing actions of this sort during verbal interaction, but rather with the explanatory power that the systematic analysis of speech acts – as these actions are customarily called – can be seen to carry with respect to fundamental epistemological questions about language, communication, or even normativity and action itself.

Given the amount of attention that speech act theory has received, it would be virtually impossible for any single treatise to cover the full breadth of perspectives that the relevant literature encompasses. The present work is no exception. In a nutshell, this Element constitutes an attempt to map the evolving relationship between speech act theory and theorising in pragmatics. Unsurprisingly, the starting point is that speech act theory is typically credited for having given birth to modern pragmatics as an independent field of enquiry; a point corroborated by the relevant literature pretty much in its entirety. As we will see, there are various important reasons – not only of conceptual, but also of historical nature – why this is so. In the first instance, though, it would be useful to justify the specific goals of the ensuing discussion. After all, speech acts feature prominently in virtually all textbooks, handbooks and encyclopaedias of pragmatics, so one might well protest that the literature already abounds with works of a similar scope.

In what is perhaps an unexpected twist, the main motivation behind this Element may actually have less to do with speech acts per se and more with the current state of theorising in pragmatics. As a look at most of the very same reference works alluded to just now attests, research in the field has been more or less anchored in two rather distinct schools of thought, which have been traditionally referred to as 'Anglo-American' and 'Continental European' pragmatics (see, e.g., Huang, 2010). Within this frame and since 'many researchers don't venture out of the comfort of their pragmatic niches, limiting their interactions to fellow-believers' (Ariel, 2010: 1), most existing overviews of speech act theory in the pragmatics literature appear to adopt the positioning of one of these two traditions (typically the Anglo-American one) from the get-go, without necessarily acknowledging the existence of the other.[1]

At the same time, speech act theory has been recognised as both 'the driving force behind the Anglo-American prominence in pragmatics' (Verschueren, 2022: 4) and a 'precursor' (Culpeper 2021: 18) to sociopragmatics, a field of enquiry of central interest for the Continental European tradition that the Anglo-American one tends to ignore. This suggests that the study of speech acts is uniquely placed when it comes to appreciating the differences between these two traditions in the discipline. Given this, this Element will approach its subject matter with a view to disentangling the effect that the evolution of pragmatic theory has had on speech act theory itself and vice versa. By doing so, it will inevitably also go over some focal points in what Jucker (2024) calls the *first wave of philosophical approaches* to the study of speech acts, complementing them with insights from later work that has shed further light to our conceptual understanding of the topic at hand. In contrast to most existing overviews which give the impression of a more or less smooth transition to a contemporary state of the art, however, the discussion here will concentrate instead on some major differences that can be encountered in the exposition of the models that have shaped this understanding.

In view of its predominantly theoretical orientation, the present work should be seen as complementary to its sister Element, *Speech Acts: Discursive, Multimodal, Diachronic* (Jucker, 2024), which focuses more acutely on empirical research on speech acts. While some of the implications of such research will also inform the present discussion, the focus here is placed instead on the explanatory power of speech act theory with a view to highlighting its contribution towards contemporary theorising in pragmatics. To this end, this Element is organised as follows: Section 2 will offer an outline of the two aforementioned traditions in pragmatics which will guide the eventual discussion, while Section 3 will introduce the subsequent theoretical grounding of speech acts. Section 4 will concentrate on the inception of speech act theory through the seminal work of Austin, with Section 5 providing an overview of its contemporary received view, as this has been formed on the basis of further elaborations on this work in Searlean and Gricean terms. Section 6 will then present the argument that, due to the domination of the Anglo-American tradition in pragmatic theorising, this received view has actually departed substantially from Austin's original vision, and Section 7 will showcase how the European-Continental alternative can help restore this vision. Finally, Section 8 will bring the discussion to a close with some brief concluding remarks.

---

[1] There are of course also notable exceptions to this trend, as in the case of Culpeper and Haugh (2014: Chapter 6) who address the topic from an *integrative* viewpoint that attempts to consolidate the two traditions.

2 Two Takes on the Scope of Pragmatics

In view of this Element's specific aim, it is necessary to start with a delineation of the scope of pragmatics, since it is within this scope that speech act theory will be considered here. Of course, as Levinson (1983: Chapter 1) masterfully showed in one of the first ever systematic overviews of the field some forty years ago, this is far from a simple task – even if one chooses to concentrate on a single take on the discipline, like Levinson did with the Anglo-American one. This situation might actually be even more complex nowadays, since, with the ever-increasing interest in the field, pragmatic research is currently being carried out from multiple different angles[2] with usually cross-cutting but sometimes also conflicting aims. As a result, there is still a very strong sense in which 'pragmatics means different things to different scholars' (Garcés-Conejos Blitvich & Sifianou, 2019: 93).

In the interest of keeping the present discussion succinct, I will have to concentrate on the conception of pragmatics put forward by the two broader schools of thought that were already identified in Section 1; something that should also be sufficient for the argument that I will eventually pursue. While doing so, however, I will refrain from referring to the relevant traditions using their aforementioned geographical labels. That is because, as Culpeper (2021: 15–16) rightly points out, these labels

> perhaps give some vague indication of where practitioners of these views are located, but disguise the variety of views held within those locations and have nothing to say about some large swathes of the world that are 'big' in pragmatics, [...] yet are neither in Continental Europe, the United Kingdom or the United States.

Instead, for reasons that will immediately become clear, I will refer to the Anglo-American tradition as the 'component' view of pragmatics and the Continental European as the 'perspective' one (following Haberland & Mey, 1977; Verschueren, 1987), additionally distinguishing between them (after Bublitz & Norrick, 2011; Culpeper & Haugh, 2014) on the basis of the breadth that each of them allocates to the scope of the discipline.

2.1 The Narrow 'Component' View

In its narrow conception, pragmatics is viewed as a *component* of our ability for language, which is to be approached on par with the other core levels of

---

[2] For instance, apart from the integrative approach mentioned in footnote 1, one can choose to engage with pragmatics from a cognitive (e.g., Wilson & Sperber, 2004), socio-cognitive (e.g., Kecskes, 2010), discursive (e.g., Garcés-Conejos Blitvich, 2024), or even variational (Schneider & Barron, 2008), inter-cultural (Kecskes, 2014) or cross-cultural (e.g., House & Kádár, 2021) angle, among several others.

linguistic analysis; that is, phonetics, phonology, morphology, syntax, and – more crucially, of course – semantics. In this picture, the focus of enquiry for pragmatics falls on the ways in which contexts of utterance can be seen to perform certain functions that complement the output of other performance systems, whose knowledge basis underlies our linguistic competence; most notably semantic interpretation, but, on occasion, morphosyntactic parsing and phonological processing too.

By and large, this view is closely linked to the mainstream way of looking at meaning in language as a function of the truth-conditional content of sentences,[3] allowing for contextual considerations to enter the picture only when necessary. From this angle, pragmatics falls under the scope of linguistic enquiry only insofar as contextual information can be shown to directly affect the semantic interpretation of sentences, like, for example, in the case of reference assignment (especially to indexicals) or disambiguation; hence its resulting characterisation as *narrow*. Indeed, even though he did advise some caution when it comes to blindly adopting this viewpoint, Levinson (1983: 32) concluded his aforementioned overview of the field's scope characterising as 'most promising' those 'definitions that equate pragmatics with "meaning minus semantics" or with a theory of language understanding that takes context into account, in order to complement the contribution that semantics makes to meaning'. Following suit, work that adopts the component orientation has tended to concentrate almost exclusively on a handful of phenomena (including, naturally, speech acts) which cannot be accounted for with resort to semantic theory alone.

This essentially 'pick-and-choose' outlook was even more evident during the early days, right before the recognition of pragmatics as a discipline in its own right. In fact, the haphazard way in which scholars would use the label 'pragmatic' back then was what famously prompted Bar-Hillel (1971: 405) to refer to pragmatics as a 'wastebasket' for linguistic phenomena which appear to not fit 'syntactico-semantic theory' and, at the same time, underline the need to 'bring some order into the contents of this wastebasket' by 'clarify[ing] somewhat better the explicandum [...] before embarking on the explication'. Understandably, such an undertaking would be neither straightforward nor easy, especially since 'an "after the fact" definition, when the set of pragmatic topics had already been relatively well established, is basically a mission impossible' (Ariel, 2010:16). As it happens though, a way of bringing this

---

[3] It is worth noting here that this outlook is firmly rooted in the tradition of formal semantics which focuses on the study of linguistic meaning in non-mentalistic terms. Even from a mentalistic viewpoint though, pragmatics is again typically viewed as an 'add-on' to semantics, conceived of this time as a 'performance theory at the semantic level' (Katz, 1977: 15).

much-needed conceptual order was already brewing, owing primarily to the collective work of Grice (1989).

Around the same time that Bar-Hillel coined the wastebasket metaphor, Grice was already developing his theory of implicature, with the express aim of accounting for the divergences in meaning that were often assumed to exist between formal devices in logic and their natural language counterparts (see, in particular, Grice, 1975). Needless to say, implicature instantly became a staple of pragmatic theory, and for good reason: not only did it help safeguard the purity of the logical approach, by allowing for a (non-truth-conditional) description of aspects of linguistic meaning that were clearly unfit for formal semantic accounts, as in the case of conventional implicatures; it also provided a principled way of explaining how contexts of utterance prototypically allow language users to communicate inferences that go beyond the standing linguistic meaning of sentences, and are thus correspondingly pragmatic in nature, as in the case of conversational implicatures.

In effect, along with the notion of a speech act, to which we will return shortly, this latter contribution of Grice also helped extend the scope of pragmatics in its narrow conception beyond its most immediate 'add-on to semantics' role. By including in the picture further inferences, especially implicatures of the particularised conversational kind, which may require linguistic meaning in order to be worked out but are still quintessentially context-driven, it drew even more attention to the study of communicated meaning. More importantly though, when it comes to the delineation of the scope of pragmatics, in developing his approach, Grice offered an ingenious solution to the aforementioned wastebasket problem. Complementing his earlier account of *nonnatural meaning* (Grice, 1957; for a brief exposition, see Section 5.3), the philosopher's theory of implicature pretty much solidified the field's emphasis on the intentions of the speaker. Adopting the Gricean rationale, research on the various distinct phenomena that, by that time, would have been taken to fall under pragmatics could now be seen to converge towards a common goal: the identification of the meaning that speakers intend to communicate to hearers when producing utterances, or as this ended up being commonly referred to, the identification of *speaker meaning*.

Overall, for scholars adopting the narrow view of the discipline, the notion of speaker meaning allowed for a clarification, as well as restriction, of the field's scope. Obviously, the interpretation of any utterance can give rise to a whole host of meaning-related inferences whose origin can be attributed to the utterance's context of production (see, e.g., Elder, 2024), but only some of those inferences are directly linked to (or derived from) the linguistic content of an utterance's underlying sentence – that is, the linguistic structure that the speaker chose to token on this specific occasion. Delimiting the focus of attention to just those contextual inferences that have been communicated *properly* – that is, by virtue of the speaker overtly inviting the hearer to draw them – would be deemed sufficient for recovering those aspects of meaning that are needed to complement the picture captured by semantic theory. As a result, with Grice's insight, the study of pragmatics in its narrow conception could finally be seen to have both a clear-cut object of investigation under the rubric of speaker meaning and a tightly knit domain of application, that of intentional verbal communication.

2.2 The Broad 'Perspective' View

As we just saw, the earliest adoptions of a pragmatic outlook for the study of language involved the operationalisation of contextual information in order to explain certain phenomena that would not fit existing semantic and syntactic accounts. Going back to the very coinage of the term 'pragmatics', however, it is easy to see that the discipline was not originally conceived of along such lines. Upon introducing the term in his seminal semiotic account, Morris (1938: 6–7) defined pragmatics as the 'study of the relation of signs to interpreters', distinguishing it from semantics and syntactics, which respectively study 'the relations of signs to the objects to which the signs are applicable' and 'the formal relation of signs to one another'. From this angle, pragmatics was expected to deal with 'the biotic aspects of semiosis, that is, with all the psychological, biological, and sociological phenomena which occur in the functioning of signs' (Morris, 1938: 30); clearly a much broader role than the one that would eventually be granted to it by the narrow pragmatics camp.

Against this backdrop, much like the narrow conception of pragmatics emerged out of a need to consolidate the scope of existing linguistic research, the broad one developed as a reaction to the way linguistic pragmatics was evolving at the time. On the occasion of launching the *Journal of Pragmatics* and in what is generally considered as the first explicit defence of the broad take on the discipline, Haberland and Mey (1977: 5) took issue with the overwhelming preoccupation of their contemporaries with 'formal pragmatics (mostly in the Montague tradition)', which they suggested may well be thought of as 'an extremely sophisticated way of doing semantics' given its complete disregard of socio-cultural considerations. According to them, since 'language, as *the* means of societal communication, is transmitted in a social setting', the human capacity for language 'cannot be studied and/or measured in the abstract' and without reference 'to the societal conditions that language learners and users live by' (Haberland & Mey, 1977: 9–10; emphasis in original). Then, drawing inspiration from Morris' original vision, and more specifically from his suggestion that pragmatic rules are to 'state the conditions in the interpreters under which the sign vehicle [in our case, some linguistic token] is a sign [i.e. meaningful]' (Morris, 1938: 35), they attributed to pragmatics the role of 'inquiring into the necessary conditions that govern the use of language' (Haberland & Mey, 1977: 6).

From then on, pragmatics would additionally be conceptualised of as a *perspective* for studying language – or, as Verschueren (2022: 14) has correspondingly put it, a 'perspective on whatever phonologists, morphologists, syntacticians, semanticists, psycholinguists, sociolinguists, etc. deal with', rather than a separate component that complements other levels of linguistic analysis. Perhaps more pertinently in view of the present discussion, embracing pragmatics 'as a general functional perspective on (any aspect of) language' essentially meant adopting 'an approach to language which takes into account the full complexity of its cognitive, social, and cultural (i.e., "meaningful") functioning in the lives of human beings' (Verschueren, 2022: 17). Given this, apart from casting a much wider net in relation to the positioning of pragmatics vis-à-vis linguistic theory, the perspective view is also deemed *broad* because it significantly extends the discipline's remit, allowing for the inclusion of multiple phenomena over and above those that the component pragmatics tradition has typically concentrated on. For instance, being generally content with delimiting their research to the domain of intentional verbal communication, the narrow-view camp has tended to disregard aspects of meaning that are not tied to speaker intentions, with 'phenomena like politeness, face-saving and turn taking' often being excluded from the remit of pragmatic analysis on the grounds that their inclusion would conflate distinct aims as to what the discipline is about (Blakemore, 1992: 47–48). By reinstating socio-cultural considerations at the centre of its agenda, the broad take on pragmatics has allowed for a 'boundless diversification' (Verschueren, 2022: 9) in the field. As a result, a significant amount of research that does not prioritise formal analysis nor concentrates specifically on the study of speaker meaning has managed to additionally flourish therein.[4]

In this picture, when it comes to the role of speaker intentions for the study of pragmatics, the perspective view casts doubt not only on their adequacy as

---

[4] On this point, an anonymous reviewer noted that the main reason why phenomena related to socio-cultural (or interactional) considerations are nowadays thought of as pragmatically-oriented, rather than simply applied, is the existence of approaches which use traditional concepts – like implicature – to explain them, as this proves unequivocally that they share something with phenomena traditionally considered to be part of pragmatics *proper*. If anything, considering also of this Element's overall aim, the observation that (many) pragmaticists would be willing to accept a topic as 'pragmatic' only if it can be somehow linked to the (theoretical concepts put forward for the) study of speaker meaning provides an additional indication of the firm grip that, as I will argue in Section 6, the narrow take on pragmatics has had on the mainstream conceptualisation of the discipline.

a defining factor for the field's object of enquiry, but also on their very traceability. As Mey and Talbot (1988: 747) note, the main problem with restricting communication to its overtly intentional dimension 'hinges on the extent to which people "know what they're doing" and the extent to which what they are doing is predetermined and even unknowable'. Again, socio-cultural considerations appear to play a central role here. Regardless of how much communicative behaviour is anchored by an individual's intentions and goals, for perspective pragmatics, it is still underlain by 'historically constituted ways of saying and doing' that a social agent 'cannot be aware of' (Mey & Talbot, 1988: 747). At the same time, drawing on conversation-analytic research that focuses on the dynamics of interaction, the broad pragmatics camp typically takes meaning to be *co-constructed* on the fly by both interlocutors through tacit negotiations that take place as a verbal exchange unravels, which in turn opens the possibility that the intentions on which verbal communication relies constitute more of 'a *post facto* participant resource that emerges through interaction' than 'an *a priori* mental state of speakers' (Haugh, 2008: 104).

All in all, the perspective take on pragmatics has attempted to shift 'the pragmatic question *par excellence*' from 'What does this utterance mean?' to 'Why has this utterance been produced?' (Haberland & Mey, 1977: 8). In this picture, the pragmaticist is called to concentrate on 'the continuous making of communicative choices, both in speaking and in interpreting' (Verschueren, 2022: 17–18); whereby these choices are by default variable, negotiated in interaction, and can be swiftly adapted to any interlocutor's communicative needs. Therefore, instead of a clear-cut object of investigation, like the traditional study of the way in which 'speakers implicate [and] hearers infer' (Horn, 2004: 6), broad pragmatics proposes an alternative way of looking at language use as a whole. From this angle, as Verschueren (2022: 19) elucidates, explanations of a pragmatic nature are to be provided within the purview of the following four guiding principles: (a) communicative choices pertain to all levels of linguistic structure; (b) the contribution of contextual factors is ever-changing and comprises socio-cultural considerations; (c) certain choices can be primed on the basis of their salience in particular situations; and (d) even communication principles and strategies can dynamically change over time.

2.3 In Lieu of a State of the Art

Even though the preceding outlines will anchor the discussion of speech act theory in what follows, it is imperative to stress that they are only indicative of a much more nuanced picture. For one, work on pragmatics that seemingly adopts either one of these two positionings abounds with variations of significant theoretical importance, such as the distinction between Grice's *speaker meaning* and relevance theory's *intended import* (Sperber & Wilson, 2015) or that between *genre* and *activity type* (Linell, 1998: Chapter 12), to name but two. Then, chances are that, confronted with a choice, scholars who self-identify as pragmaticists would only accept being categorised as working solely within one of these two traditions with some pretty hefty caveats. For instance, the vast majority of research that adopts the perspective view of pragmatics still relies heavily on theoretical concepts and analytical distinctions that were originally drawn with a view to accounting for speaker meaning in encapsulation from socio-cultural or interactional considerations. Similarly, approaches that have traditionally been couched in a narrow-view background do not always shy away from taking into account such considerations either, as can be seen, for instance, in the incorporation of a full-fledged conversation-analytic approach to the treatment of speech acts in Levinson (1983, 2017; see also Section 7.2) or in recent work on relevance theory that seeks to draw the focus away from speaker intentions (Assimakopoulos, 2021a, 2022). Therefore, as Culpeper and Haugh (2014: 7) rightly point out, 'one should not over-emphasise differences between the [...two] views'.

Still, given their obvious points of divergence, looking at how these views approach the scope of the field can be useful in assessing its evolution. To wit, narrow pragmatics takes linguistic representations as its point of departure with a view to accounting for those meaning-related phenomena that cannot be fully approached in abstraction from their context of utterance. In contrast, broad pragmatics adopts a *top-down* approach, in the specific sense that it starts from society and the interlocutors themselves and concentrates on how the conditions of the former and the patterns of interaction of the latter shape the context that mediates meaning-making on all occasions of language use. By the same token, each tradition relies on a rather different conception of context, too. In component pragmatics, we typically talk about *utterance contexts*, concentrating mainly on those aspects of contextual information which reveal the meaning that the speaker intended to communicate on some occasion of use or another.[5] Conversely, for perspective pragmatics, the focus is placed on the broader

---

[5] According to an anonymous reviewer, even within the component view, scholars like Bach have drawn a distinction between narrow and broad context, with the latter containing much of what is attributed to the perspective view here. However, as Bach himself (2012: 156; emphasis my own) puts it, 'broad context includes *the information that the speaker exploits to make what she means evident to the hearer* and, if communication is to succeed, that the hearer takes into account, on the assumption that *he is intended to figure out what the speaker means*'. So, even though intentions are not completely a-social and can be shaped by sociocultural norms in this picture too, this dimension seems, again, to be taken into account only when it becomes relevant for the identification of speaker meaning in the technical sense of the term.

discourse context,[6] which focuses instead on all stages of a communicative exchange and includes the vast range of socio-cultural norms and attitudes that underlie them, affecting both interlocutors' behaviour. Finally, differences can also be located even in the methodological choices of scholars subscribing to the two camps, as is evident in the insistence of researchers adopting the broad view of pragmatics to work on authentic sequences of verbal interaction, when corresponding work on narrow pragmatics has traditionally relied on the analysis of single utterances in invented question-answer pairs.

In conclusion, appreciating the caution that Culpeper and Haugh have advised, perhaps the safest way to approach the distinction at hand is by following Haberland and Mey (2002: 1674) in viewing component and perspective pragmatics as two 'extremes', whereby 'narrow but precise description' is respectively juxtaposed with 'broad but fuzzy inclusion'. Clearly, being extremes, they both have their weaknesses when taken at face value, with narrow pragmatics appearing too restrictive to many and broad pragmatics being correspondingly deemed 'too inclusive to be of much use' (Davis, 1991: 3) to others. Still, as we will eventually see, they are both extremely useful when it comes to the theoretical description of speech acts.

3 Speech Act Theory: Setting the Scene

Virtually all meaningful utterances we produce as we go about our daily lives can be taken to constitute goal-oriented actions, like apologies, requests, warnings, invitations, or even mere assertions, as per the corresponding examples in (1)–(5). In effect, it is these actions that are performed by meaningful utterances while we interact with our peers that the literature refers to as speech acts.

1. *I am sorry I'm late.*
2. *Could you open the door?*
3. *Watch out, the floor is slippery!*
4. *How about we go for a walk?*
5. *My favourite colour is blue.*

While the notion of a speech act should be intuitively easy to grasp, when it comes to the way in which scholars have theorised about it, a situation similar to what we just encountered with respect to pragmatics appears to present itself. Even as far back as thirty years ago, Weigand (1996: 367) would comment,

---

[6] The use of the label 'discourse context' here is meant to capture an extended and dynamic conception of context 'as the continually changing surroundings, in the widest sense, that enable the participants in the communication process to interact, and in which the linguistic expressions of their interaction become intelligible' (Mey, 2001: 39). It should thus not be confused with the highly formalised notion of 'discourse context' that is put forth in different variations of dynamic semantics.

> from its beginning, speech act theory has undergone a series of developments.... However, there is ... no foundation for speech act theory in the sense of a generally accepted consistent theory. We have some models: Austin, Searle in different versions, Grice and others. Their assumptions do not form a unified whole, to a certain extent they even contradict each other.

Obviously, this is something that has affected speech act theory's reception within pragmatics too. The average overview of speech acts in the relevant literature typically starts by identifying their theoretical basis as the brainchild of Austin and making special reference to Searle for clarifying and further systematising Austin's original proposal. From then on, the ideas of the two philosophers are usually mingled, with relatively little juxtaposition, while, at the same time, the role of speaker intentions is also thrown into the mix with a view to explaining how speech acts can be approached in terms of pragmatic inference.

Circling back to the discussion in Section 2, this suggests that, while research in both traditions in pragmatics makes extensive reference to speech acts (as intentional acts from the component angle and social actions from the perspective one), their theoretical explanation is predominantly aligned with the narrow take on the discipline. As already mentioned, a main aim of this Element is to challenge this received view, by drawing attention to the possibility that the original exposition of speech act theory may actually be closer in spirit to the broad view of pragmatics than the relevant literature acknowledges. To use a justification that Sbisà (2007: 461) has also put forth, albeit in relation to a different matter, the main reason for this is that 'Austin's original proposal has often been conflated with subsequent versions of speech act theory', and at the same time 'there have been early misreadings of it, which have been extremely influential'. Of course, any general overview of speech act theory should necessarily incorporate the findings of such versions too, so this is something that we will return to in Section 5. Given our aforementioned aim, however, it is essential in the first instance to not lose sight of the original argumentation through which speech acts were introduced as a theoretical construct.

4 The Inception of Speech Act Theory

The origin of speech act theory is typically located in Austin's *How to Do Things with Words* (1962/1975), a posthumous publication of the notes that the philosopher used when delivering his William James Lectures at Harvard University in 1955. Obviously, Austin was not at all concerned with carving a theory of pragmatics; rather, his postulation of speech acts was born out of an interest in questions pertaining to the description of language within the remit of analytic philosophy, a topic of central interest among philosophers of language at the time.

As is well known, analytic philosophy 'has especially emphasized the ideal of clarity and pursued exactness by means of logical and mathematical tools' (Haaparanta, 2013: 3). Around roughly the middle of the previous century, when Austin also engaged with the field, there was already a long-established tradition of the so-called *ideal language philosophy*, infatuated with the analytical precision that formal logic offers when it comes to modelling meaning and reasoning. Seeing how this approach was capable of solving several philosophical puzzles pertaining to natural language as well, philosophers of this orientation would increasingly rely on logic in their work on that domain too. Reacting to this trend, however, another group, dubbed *ordinary language philosophers* this time, would protest that 'important features of natural language were not revealed but hidden by the logical approach' (Recanati, 2004a: 442), and therefore sought alternative ways to account for these features.[7]

It is evident right from the beginning of Austin's lecture series that his proposed account was intended to problematise and highlight precisely such a feature. As Austin himself (1975: 1) put it, it had already been 'for too long the assumption of philosophers that the business of a "statement" can only be to "describe" some state of affairs, or to "state some fact", which it must do either truly or falsely'. Here, reference was made to the ideal language tradition's tendency to equate the meaning of any natural language sentence with its propositional content; a tendency that, as we also saw in Section 2.1, has been inherited by contemporary formal semantic theory too and, thus, lies at the heart of the rationale underlying the component view of pragmatics. From this angle, knowing the meaning of a sentence amounts to knowing the conditions that need to obtain in the world for it to be true. So, the propositional content of a sentence like '*Snow is white.*', to use Tarski's (1944) famous example, can be captured in its entirety by specifying the state of affairs that would need to hold in order for a statement of the sentence to be true (in the sense that the object denoted by the word *snow* 'satisfies' the property denoted by the word *white*). With the advent of the philosophical movement of logical positivism, however, this position reached extreme interpretations, including even the conclusion that statements which cannot be evaluated for their truth or falsity are essentially meaningless (see, e.g., Ayer, 1936).

Against this background, Austin's reaction came under the guise of what he called the *descriptive fallacy*. Seeing how the focus of enquiry for philosophers of language had started to fall exclusively on the specification of the meaning of truth-evaluable declarative sentences, the philosopher systematically argued

---

[7] For a succinct overview of the evolution of the philosophical interest in the study of language and meaning, see Chapman (2006: Chapter 4).

that the function of linguistic utterances goes far beyond this descriptive dimension. To fully appreciate his position, however, it is important to get acquainted with the admittedly complex argumentation by which he introduced his theory of speech acts.

4.1 From Performatives ...

The first part of Austin's lecture series motivates the concept of the descriptive fallacy by drawing attention to the fact that there are several commonly used utterances which remain meaningful despite having a primary function that quite clearly deviates from the mere description of states of affairs. In contrast to *constatives*, which is what Austin (1975: 7) called descriptive statements that are 'normally thought of as just saying something', what the philosopher had in mind here is a specific group of utterances that can be quite straightforwardly seen to be 'doing something' (Austin, 1975: 12) instead. For example, consider the following:

6. *I promise that I will come to your party.*
7. *I apologise for having kept you waiting.*
8. *I order you to wash the dishes.*
9. *I sentence you to 5 years in prison.*

Even intuitively, it should be pretty easy to see that the primary aim of the utterances in (6)-(9) is quite different from providing a simple description of a state of affairs; rather, they explicitly seek to perform an action – be it making a promise, as in (6), an apology, as in (7), a command, as in (8), or giving someone a prison sentence, as in (9). In view of this, Austin fittingly called utterances of this sort *performatives* and dedicated roughly the first half of his lecture series to exploring how they can be identified in contradistinction to constatives.

When it comes to the mechanics of performative utterances, Austin showed that an utterance does not really need to embed a special verb, like '*sentence*', '*promise*', '*apologise*', or '*order*', in order to constitute a performative. Utterances of this sort can also be produced without such *performative verbs*, as in (10), which can pretty straightforwardly substitute (6) when uttered in the same context.

10. *I will come to your party.*

Along these lines, apart from *explicit performative utterances* like the ones in (6)–(9), Austin recognised the existence of *implicit* ones too, which carry out pretty much the same types of actions. At the same time, he also acknowledged that the mere presence of what appears to be a performative verb in an utterance does not really guarantee the utterance's performative character, since verbs of this class can also be used *non-performatively*. Consider, for instance, a context in which I am producing the utterance in (11), while recounting a hypothetical scene from the movie *Titanic*, in which Jack momentarily leaves Rose to go save a little boy from drowning.

11. *Jack promised Rose that he will find her.*

In uttering (11), I am clearly not engaging in an act of promise myself; I am rather reporting on such an act having being performed by Jack, by producing a statement that is ultimately describing a state of affairs which can either be true, if Jack indeed made that promise, or false otherwise. Similarly, the same class of verbs can also be used non-performatively when describing habitual behaviour, as in the case of (12).

12. *I promise only when I know I can keep my word.*

On top of 'the verbs which seem, on grounds of vocabulary, to be specially performative verbs' (1975, p. 61), Austin also considered a number of additional ways in which the performative function of the relevant utterance class can be identified, but again found them all wanting. For one, as shown by the example utterances in (13a) and (13b), which could be used interchangeably to perform the same action, person and voice are immaterial in this context.

13. a. *I am letting you go.*
    b. *You are fired.*

Then, while typically a good criterion for establishing an utterance's function, sentence mood was deemed inappropriate too, since there is no one-to-one relation between the form of a sentence and the performative function of its utterance. For example, someone could well advise me to stop smoking by using the explicit indicative sentence in (14a), but they could also do the same by using the conditional in (14b).

14. a. *I advise you to stop smoking.*
    b. *If I were you, I would stop smoking.*

The same applies to tense. As we can see in the case of (15b), which can perform the same action as (15a) even though it uses the past instead of the present tense, as performatives typically tend to do, tense does not always provide a reliable indication of a performative function,

15. a. *I find you guilty of breaking that vase.*
    b. *You broke that vase.*

Despite the apparent difficulty in identifying a linguistic or grammatical criterion that can reveal an utterance's performative character at face value, Austin's exploration did not leave him entirely empty-handed either. It still provided him with a blueprint for prototypical explicit performatives, enabling him to consider the possibility that any 'performative should be reducible, or expandible, or analysable into a form, or reproducible in a form, with a verb in the first person singular present indicative active' (Austin, 1975: 61–62), as per our examples (6)–(9). Even though this *explicit performative formula* does not really guarantee the presence of a performative utterance, as we saw in (12), it can be particularly useful for reframing an implicit performative in explicit terms; simply consider the reformulation of our example in (10) into that in (6). At that, an extra step that can help confirm whether we are in the presence of a pure performative utterance would be to insert the adverb '*hereby*' between the verb and the subject in this formula: if the insertion is permissible, as in (16), the verb is used performatively; if not, as in (17), the utterance can be classified as descriptive.

16. *I hereby promise that I will come to your party.*
17. **I hereby promise only when I know I can keep my word.*

4.1.1 Conditions for Felicitous Performance

Naturally, Austin's investigation of the constative/performative distinction did not just concentrate on the form of the relevant utterances. A substantial part of his account also dealt with the relative contribution of performatives, as opposed to constatives, to the speech situations in which they arise. As we saw in (11), while the propositional content of an utterance that reports on a performative can be evaluated as true or false, asking whether the content of an act of this sort itself can be assigned a truth value is very much beside the point. Consider, for example, the utterance in (18), as directed by Jack to Rose in the same context hypothesised in (11).

18. *I will find you.*

Quite evidently, the extent to which the proposition expressed in (18) can be evaluated for its truth is pretty much irrelevant. Rather, the only aspect of its meaning that could conceivably be judged as true or false in this context is whether the expression of this proposition constitutes an act of promise on the part of Jack.

With truth conditions becoming immaterial in this setting, approaching the relevant contribution of performatives is bound to need a different handle. As

Austin (1975: 14) noted in this vein, 'besides the uttering of the words of the so-called performative, a good many other things have as a general rule to be right and to go right if we are to be said to have happily brought off our action'. Indeed, since performatives are themselves actions, the right question to ask, instead of whether they are true or false, is whether the action they perform has been successfully executed. To this end, Austin (1975: 14–15), suggested a number of conditions that a performative needs to satisfy in order to fulfil its function:

- A. (1) There must exist an accepted conventional procedure having a certain conventional effect, that procedure to include the uttering of certain words by certain persons in certain circumstances, and further, (2) the particular persons and circumstances in a given case must be appropriate for the invocation of the particular procedure invoked.
- B. (1) The procedure must be executed by all participants both correctly and (2) completely.
- Γ. (1) Where, as often, the procedure is designed for use by persons having certain thoughts or feelings, or for the inauguration of certain consequential conduct on the part of any participant, then a person participating in and so invoking the procedure must in fact have those thoughts or feelings, and the participants must intend so to conduct themselves, and further (2) must actually so conduct themselves subsequently.

Austin's categorisation of these conditions into three pairs was meant to highlight the different ways in which performative utterances can fail to complete their associated action, which would ultimately render them 'unhappy', as the philosopher himself put it (Austin, 1975: 15): the conditions under A and B are meant to capture the successful performance of an action, while those under Γ control for cases where the deployment of the performative utterance may be successful but is at the same time defective, inappropriate or misleading. In this picture, when an infelicity is due to non-adherence to a condition under A and B, we have a *misfire* of a purported performative, whereas when this infelicity results from a violation of Γ, we are in the presence of an *abuse* of a performative which has otherwise been successfully launched.

In order to see how these conditions work in practice, let's consider some scenarios in which they would be taken to not be observed. In relation to condition A.1, suppose that you want to insult someone, but instead of just using any one of the many conventional ways to do so (directly or by resorting to sarcasm, a joke, a slur, etc.), you merely utter (19).

19. *I insult you.*

Despite your original intention to perform the relevant action, chances are that the action will not be completed, since the verb '*insult*' is conventionally descriptive, rather than performative. Turning to condition A.2, imagine a situation in which two siblings fight and one tells the other: '*I sentence you to 5 years in prison.*', as in (9) further up. Here, the speaker may have indeed used a conventional (almost ritualistic) procedure for performing the action at hand, but given the circumstances, and more specifically their lack of the relevant authority to send anyone, let alone their interlocutor, to prison, the action itself is void, or, as Austin put it, *misapplied*. All in all, on both these occasions of a misfire, the infelicity can be taken to result from what Austin called a *misinvocation* of procedure.

Along similar lines, infelicities due to the two conditions in B are the result of a *misexecution* of the performative, since they arise when there are *flaws* (B.1) or *hitches* (B.2) in performing the relevant action. Flaws relate to an otherwise appropriate application of a conventional procedure for the act itself, which, however, includes a mistake; as when a priest utters (20) during a wedding ceremony, but the names of the couple getting married are actually '*John*' and '*Mary*'.

20. *Bill and Kate, I now pronounce you husband and wife.*

Hitches, on the other hand, have to do with issues that may impede the complete performance of the purported action. For example, I may utter (21) genuinely intending to offer a bet, but unless you somehow acknowledge that this is the case, the bet is not really on.

21. *I bet you my lunch money that we will win tonight's game.*

Finally, when it comes to violations of the conditions under Γ, that is, *abuses* of the performative, these apply to situations where the verbal invocation of the action may have been successful, but its performance is still infelicitous due to a lack of the appropriate psychological states on the part of the speaker or simply because the parties involved do not really follow through with it. Such abuses can be seen to take place on the grounds of *insincerities* (Γ.1) when, for example, someone promises to do something without having any intention to keep their promise. Similarly, in our familiar example of offering a bet, a performative can be taken to have been abused if, despite both interlocutors having previously explicitly agreed on it, one of them still does not keep their end of the agreement (Γ.2).

All in all, by introducing the constative/performative distinction, Austin did not just challenge the dominant view of his time, which concentrated almost exclusively on the descriptive dimension of the meaning of sentences; he

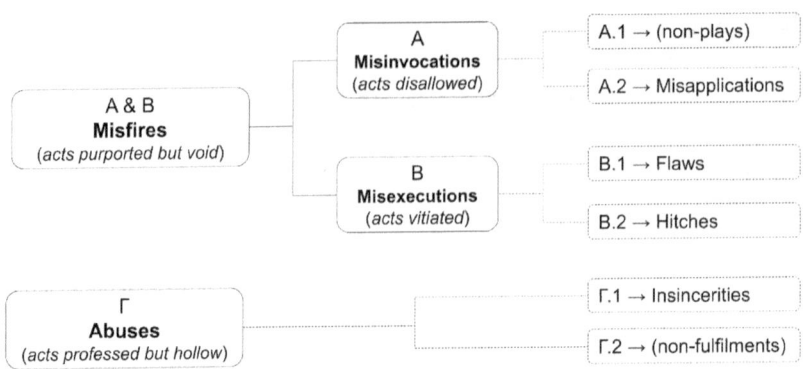

Figure 1 The doctrine of infelicities (after Austin, 1975: 18)

essentially showed that the primary function of a great deal of utterances that are ubiquitously produced out of our linguistic repertoire is to do, rather than describe things. At that, he offered a principled way of accounting for the way in which utterances of this kind remain meaningful, by identifying the conditions that ensure their successful performance. Through this *doctrine of infelicities* (summarised in Figure 1), Austin further substantiated what it means for an utterance to execute an action, providing a detailed account of the ways in which the actions that the relevant utterances perform may fail to be realised. Still, as we will now turn to see, Austin's contribution runs much deeper than the identification of just a special class of utterances whose content necessitates an alternative approach to capturing their essence.

4.2 ... to speech acts

Halfway through his argumentation, Austin's own inquiry into the opposition between constatives and performatives led him to altogether question the relevant distinction. What prompted him to seek, as he himself put it, 'a fresh start on the problem' was the failure, as per the foregoing discussion, 'to find a grammatical criterion for performatives' (Austin, 1975: 91), alongside the realisation that even descriptive statements can be straightforwardly reformulated into explicit performatives by means of the explicit performative formula, without this actually compromising their being truth-evaluable. Consider, for example, the relevant reformulation of our prototypical constative utterance in (22a) into an explicit performative in (22b):

22. a. *Snow is white.*
    b. *I (hereby) state/assert/suggest ... that snow is white.*

By the same token, Austin additionally recognised that, by effectively performing an act of asserting or stating,[8] constatives too have conditions for felicitous performance, in the sense that they can also misfire or be abused. For instance, my production of (23) at this very moment would easily be seen as a misinvocation of the procedure for asserting, since I quite obviously have no way of knowing, let alone asserting, that the exact number I mention is correct.

23. *There are 10,323 babies being born around the world right now.*

Similarly, assertions can also be misexecuted, as is often the case with slips of the tongue, such as in (24), where '*penguins*' is quite clearly used by mistake in the place of '*pigeons*'.

24. *Mary is feeding the penguins in Hyde Park.*

Finally, insofar as a 'statement is liable to the insincerity form of infelicity' (Austin, 1975: 136), assertions are equally liable to abuses of type Γ, as in the case of (25), when uttered by someone who has not actually engaged in the relevant action:

25. *I processed the refund to your account two days ago.*

Showing, then, that even constatives can be seen to operate on par with performatives, Austin reached the conclusion that all utterances should effectively be considered as action and are thus amenable to the treatment that had up to that point been reserved for the discussion of performatives alone; hence the reappraisal of all utterances as speech acts from this point of his argumentation onwards.

4.2.1 The Dimensions of a Speech Act

In putting forward his account of speech acts, Austin argued that, when looking at language use as action, the production of an utterance should be conceived of as a complex act that can be approached from three distinct aspects. For one, there is the *locutionary act*, which is essentially the act of producing an utterance with intelligible meaning, or as the philosopher himself put it, the act of simply 'saying something' (Austin, 1975: 94).[9] Then, we have the *illocutionary act* which corresponds to what Austin had previously identified as the

---

[8] Stating and asserting are of course distinct actions – and this is something that Austin clearly recognised (see, in particular, Austin, 1953). However, given the present space restrictions and since this specific distinction will not play any central role in my argumentation, I have opted to refer to them interchangeably for ease of exposition.

[9] Notably, while describing the locutionary act, Austin suggested that it can be further broken down into a *phonetic*, a *phatic* and a *rhetic* act, whereby the first refers to the action of producing sounds, the second to the action of putting these sounds together into organised words and the third to the action of attributing to this string of words some appropriate referential meaning.

performative and thus relates to the action performed through the production of a meaningful utterance (i.e., the locution), as in the case of requesting, promising, or simply making an assertion. In this context, Austin referred to the purpose of the utterance, or – to put it more aptly – the 'type [...] of function' (1975: 100) that the utterance fulfils, as its *illocutionary force*, which is also that aspect of a speech act that gives it its name. Finally, the third broad action that language users engage in when producing utterances is the *perlocutionary act*, which is the act of bringing about 'certain consequential effects upon the feelings, thoughts, or actions of the audience, or of the speaker, or of other persons' (Austin, 1975: 101). Considering the aforementioned examples of illocutionary forces then, such effects would include the target of a request opting to engage in an action that fulfils it (or not), the acceptance on behalf of the listener (or even a by-stander) of the commitment of the speaker to follow through with a promise, or the impact that an assertion can have on its audience.

To give an example, consider the utterance of (26), as directed by a teenage boy to his mother in what should be a rather familiar context, or the utterance of (27) in a hypothetical context where Peter is talking to Mary about his new colleague, John.

26. *Close the door!*
27. *John is married.*

By our previous standards, (26) would have qualified as a performative, while (27) as a constative. From the present angle though, both are to be approached as speech acts which comprise all the aforementioned dimensions, as follows:

28. In the context of (26), the teenager performs the acts of
    - Locution: He said '*Close the door!*' to his mother.
    - Illocution: He ordered his mother to close the door.
    - Perlocution: He got his mother to close the door.

29. In the context of (27), Peter performs the acts of
    - Locution: He said '*John is married.*' to Mary.
    - Illocution: He asserted that John is married.
    - Perlocution: He brought to Mary's attention that John is married.[10]

---

[10] To be fair, Austin (1975: 139–140) did consider the possibility that 'there is no perlocutionary object specifically associated with stating, as there is with informing, arguing, etc.', but concluded that this 'would not justify giving [...] "descriptions" [any ...] priority', since the same 'is in any case true of many illocutionary acts'. Given this, I have opted to identify this assertion's perlocutionary effect as generically as possible, by referring to the way in which, when understood, a statement impinges on the hearer's attention. Obviously, beyond that, there may be further perlocutionary effects too.

4.2.2 Distinguishing between the Dimensions of a Speech Act

In line with his overall focus on what had by now become the performative character of language use in general, Austin's explicit aim in the second part of his lecture series was to 'fasten on the second, illocutionary act and contrast it with the other two' (1975: 103). In this regard, even his choice of terminology can be quite informative. An *il*locution signifies the 'performance of an act *in* saying something as opposed to performance of an act *of* saying something' which is the locution's remit, while a *per*locution refers to the eventual effects that come about *by* saying something (Austin, 1975: 99–100; emphasis in original). Simply put, for any speech act, the locution captures the act of producing a meaningful utterance, the illocution the function of this utterance in the communicative exchange, and the perlocution the generation of practical or psychological effects that are consequences of this utterance's meaning and force. Since the relevant distinctions are of central importance to the theoretical discussion of speech acts and will also substantially inform the argumentation eventually put forth in this Element, it is important to zoom in on them a bit more.

Let's start with the difference between locution and illocution. Clearly, the question that immediately presents itself when constatives are included in the performative mix concerns the place of Austin's conditions for successful performance vis-à-vis traditional truth conditions when it comes to approaching an utterance's contribution to the speech situation; after all, as we saw in Section 4.1, by Austin's previous standards, descriptive statements were to be distinguished from performatives on the grounds of their truth-conditional content, but in the new picture, utterances that were previously considered constatives both 'satisfy the requirements of being performative [...] and surely are essentially true or false' (Austin, 1975: 91). The answer to this question can be located in a comment that Austin made towards the end of his lecture series, during the provision of an 'objective assessment of the accomplished utterance' (Austin, 1975: 140). Here, despite having essentially abandoned the constative/performative distinction by that point, the philosopher further elucidated that 'with the constative utterance, we abstract from the illocutionary (let alone the perlocutionary) aspects of the speech act, and we concentrate on the locutionary', while 'with the performative utterance, we attend as much as possible to the illocutionary force of the utterance, and abstract from the dimension of correspondence with facts', which is to be associated with the locutionary (Austin, 1975: 144–145). Noting the link between the traditional truth-conditional approach to the study of meaning and Austin's reference to 'the dimension of correspondence with facts', it is easy to see how, in contrast to illocutions which concentrate on an utterance's force, locutions are the loci of 'the truth/falsehood dimension' (Austin, 1975: 148). So, roughly speaking, with respect to our example of an assertion in (27) and its speech-act-theoretic analysis in (29), the expression of the (truth-evaluable) utterance '*John is married*' would be the product of the locutionary act, with that of the illocutionary act being the reception of the utterance as carrying the force of a statement.

Evidently, a main merit of this distinction is that it allows us to explain how uttering the same sentence can carry distinct illocutionary forces in different contexts. Let's consider, for example, possible utterances of our familiar sentence '*I will find you*'. As we saw in (18), where Jack directed such an utterance to Rose in our hypothetical scene of the *Titanic*, it carried the force of a promise – or at least commitment on the part of Jack. In a different context, however, such as when produced by Bryan Mills while he is talking on the phone to his daughter's kidnappers in the movie *Taken*, it can be straightforwardly taken to carry the force of a threat. Obviously, it should not be too hard to think of different contexts where the utterance of the same sentence can carry other illocutionary forces too. So, by distinguishing between the locutionary and the illocutionary acts, Austin effectively showed how performing a single locution can actually give rise to different illocutions as a function of the context in which the locution is produced.

Turning to the way in which the illocutionary and the perlocutionary act differ from each other, Austin's take on the matter (1975: 103; emphasis in original) was that 'the former may, for rough contrast, be said to be *conventional*, in the sense that at least it could be made explicit by the performative formula; but the latter could not'. To exemplify, let's consider the command in (26) and its speech-act-theoretic analysis in (28). Evidently, the illocutionary act in this case can be straightforwardly reformulated into the explicit (albeit, rather socially awkward) performative in (30), in a way that the corresponding perlocutionary act in (31) cannot:

30. *I (hereby) order you to close the door.*
31. **I (hereby) get you to close the door.*

According to Austin (1975: 103–104), the same appears to be the case when applying the explicit performative formula to most other illocution/perlocution pairs too: 'we can say "*I argue that*" or "*I warn you that*" but we cannot say "*I convince you that*", or "*I alarm you that*"'. As follows from this, illocutionary forces can be communicated explicitly with the use of a relevant performative verb, whereas their eventual consequences, which are covered by the perlocution, can only be communicated in descriptive terms, as, for example, in (32), which reports on the perlocutionary effect of our familiar command:

32. *I got my mother to close the door (by ordering her)*.

The performative formula may indeed offer a useful way of telling illocutions and perlocutions apart, but it does not, at face value at least, provide us with any significant insight about the theoretical distinction under question (although, see Sbisà, 2009: 47–49). In order to gain such insight, we need to focus for a moment on how Austin uses the – admittedly theoretically-charged – term 'conventional' in this setting. As you may recall, this is not the first time that we have encountered this term in the present overview. Austin also used it when laying out the conditions for a performative's successful performance, where he posited that what we have now identified as the illocutionary force of a speech act is felicitous only if it follows 'an accepted conventional procedure having a certain conventional effect'. In this context, a conventional procedure is customarily assumed to refer to the means by which illocutions are performed, in the sense of typical ways in which language users make requests, promises, assertions and the like through specific locutions; hence the equation of an illocution to 'an act done as conforming to a convention' (Austin, 1975: 105).

When it comes to conventional effects, however, the situation is more complex. As we have seen, Austin defined perlocutions as yielding 'certain consequential effects upon the feelings, thoughts, or actions of the audience, or of the speaker, or of other persons'; yet, in his doctrine of infelicities, he also made reference to conventional effects, which this time apply to the level of illocution instead. Given this, what makes 'the distinction between illocutions and perlocutions [...] likeliest to give trouble' (Austin, 1975: 110) is the need to distinguish between a speech act's different kinds of effects.

This is where yet another central notion, that of *uptake*, enters the picture. Generally speaking, the difference between the conventional effects of an illocution and the consequential effects of a perlocution lies in the very nature of each respective act itself. To wit, illocution may set an expectation for the achievement of some specific consequence (that is, the consequence that this illocution typically – or conventionally – brings about), but it is perlocution that brings about any eventual, 'real production of real effects' (Austin, 1975: 103).[11] For instance, in our well-worn example in (26), the teenager can be said to have achieved the relevant perlocutionary effect through his utterance, only if his mother heard his utterance and took it 'in a certain sense' (Austin, 1975: 116). If she had not taken it in this sense, that is, as having the force of a command with all its associated conventional effects, the illocutionary act

---

[11] As Sbisà (2024: 31) aptly puts it, 'illocutionary acts have conventional states of affairs as their effects, while the effects of perlocutionary acts are psychological states, attitudes, or stretches of actual behaviour'.

would have been infelicitous. That is because, even if she did decide to close the door out of her own accord, this would not have been because the teenager got her to close it *by* ordering her to do so. It is in this spirit that Austin posited that the felicitous 'performance of an illocutionary act involves the securing of *uptake*'; that is, 'the understanding of the meaning and of the force of the locution' (Austin, 1975: 117), as well as the recognition of the typical effects it customarily brings about (on this, see also Section 6.2). Once uptake is secured and these typical effects are recognised, their actual fulfilment is a product of the perlocution.

4.2.3 Austin's Classification of Illocutionary Forces

Having replaced the constative/performative distinction with an overarching theory of speech acts and explored the main differences between the dimensions of the latter, in his concluding lecture, Austin sought to distinguish among different kinds of illocutionary forces. Assuming that illocutionary forces can be made explicit through the use of the performative formula, his strategy for coming up with the relevant categories was by grouping together different types of performative verbs on the basis of some main features of the illocutionary forces they designate.

Within this frame, the first category that he posited is that of *verdictives* which consist in 'acts of delivering of a finding, official or unofficial, upon evidence or reasons' (Austin, 1975: 153), such as when acquitting and convicting or when rating, estimating, assessing, and so on. Then, we have the category of *exercitives* which comprises acts that engage in 'the giving of a decision in favour of or against a certain course of action' (Austin, 1975: 155), like ordering, announcing, pleading, resigning, and so on, and differ from verdictives on the grounds that they deliver decisions rather than judgements. The third category is that of *commissives*, whose function is 'to commit the speaker to a certain course of action' (Austin, 1975: 157), and thus includes acts of promising, undertaking, betting, and the like. The fourth includes *behabitives*, which constitute acts 'of reaction to other people's behaviour and fortunes and of attitudes and expressions of attitudes to someone else's past conduct or imminent conduct' (Austin, 1975: 160), like apologising, complimenting, welcoming, protesting, and so on. Finally, the fifth and clearly most populated category in the mix is that of *expositives* which comprises acts that 'make plain how our utterances fit into the course of an argument or conversation' (Austin, 1975: 152), and thus involve 'the expounding of views, the conducting of arguments, and the clarifying of usages and of references' (Austin, 1975: 161), as when we affirm, deny, remark, agree, report, and so on.

4.3 How to Read Austin

As should have become evident by now, the complexity of Austin's original argumentation lies primarily in his decision to inaugurate his discussion with the description of a special class of utterances whose treatment is not amenable to a truth-conditional analysis, but then eventually extend the relevant rationale to the treatment of all utterances over and above this – initially introduced as special – class. Indeed, this is something that was criticised by several of Austin's contemporaries, while even nowadays, Austin is typically thought to have simply changed his mind about pursuing the constative/performative distinction while he was developing his argumentation. As a result, most overviews of speech act theory in the pragmatics literature, tend to only refer to it in passing, concentrating on the philosopher's eventual description of speech acts instead, which is again only briefly presented before his views are mixed with later elaborations on the topic.

Against this backdrop, the main reason why this Element has dedicated substantially more space to Austin's original argumentation than other related overviews of speech act theory is that it will eventually return to this argumentation with a view to challenging the mainstream way of theorising about speech acts nowadays. Granted, as we will see in Section 6, Austin's exposition may have had some exegetical weaknesses, such as his lack of clarity or precision in the use of theoretically-charged terms at times, but lack of coherence should not be considered one of them. As Sbisà (2007: 462–463) elucidates in a paper which also inspired the heading of the present subsection, there is actually 'no trace of a change of mind in the various sets of [Austin's] notes forming the manuscript'; rather, *How to Do Things with Words* should be read as 'a complex argument in support of the claim that all speech should be considered as action and, more specifically, that speech can be described as the performing of actions of the same kind as those performed by means of performative utterances'.

5 The Received View of Speech Act Theory in Pragmatics

As already mentioned, while all pragmaticists recognise Austin's seminal role in the shaping of speech act theory and unequivocally use his tripartite approach to speech acts, there are also further elaborations from subsequent work, especially by Austin's student, Searle, that have grown to be considered key for modern pragmatic theory. At that, even though he was not engaged with pragmatic theory per se either, Searle (1969: 16) did pinpoint the way in which speech acts quintessentially underlie the scope of the field:

> The reason for concentrating on the study of speech acts is simply this: all linguistic communication involves linguistic acts. The unit of the linguistic communication is not, as has generally been supposed, the symbol, word, or

sentence, or even the token of the symbol, word, or sentence, but rather the production or issuance of the symbol or word or sentence in the performance of the speech act. [... S]peech acts [...] are the basic or minimal unit of linguistic communication.

From this angle, once we define pragmatics as the study of meaning in linguistic communication and accept that the production of any utterance during verbal interaction is essentially a speech act, it follows that, when engaging with pragmatic analysis, what we are effectively dealing with is always a speech act. Quite crucially, this observation holds regardless of whether one prefers the narrow or the broad take on the discipline; that is, regardless of whether one favours a conception of speech acts as intentional or social actions respectively. Still, as repeatedly noted in the foregoing discussion, most overviews of speech act theory within the pragmatics literature tend to present its theoretical underpinnings along the lines of the narrow take on the discipline. Without breaking with tradition then, the following presentation of the currently *received view* of speech act theory in the field will also adopt the outlook of narrow pragmatics.

5.1 Speech Act Theory and Component Pragmatics

As already mentioned in Section 2.1, before being recognised as a discipline in its own right, pragmatics would be casually included in formal analyses on an as-needed basis. For component pragmatics, what speech act theory did was pretty much eliminate this optionality. By accepting that all utterances are effectively speech acts, an extra layer of illocutionary force would always have to be added over and above that of propositional content, when it comes to their description. So, even though one might have in principle been able to argue that meaning can be studied in its entirety through the lens of formal theory up to that point, the same could not be said for illocutionary force, given its obvious context-dependence. To put it simply, since all utterances have an illocutionary force – some even explicitly so – and the analysis of this force necessitates input from pragmatics, then pragmatics needs to be recognised as a compulsory part of linguistic analysis.

In this picture, the aspect of speech act theory that has featured most prominently in the disciplinary conceptualisation of pragmatics is the distinction between an utterance's content and its force. In fact, this distinction is so fundamental that it even underlies a most popular way of altogether distinguishing between semantics and pragmatics, whereby 'semantics studies the contents of communicative acts [... and] pragmatics studies their force' (Green, 2021: section 2.1). The relevant literature typically attributes this distinction to Austin and the way in which he correspondingly distinguished between the locutionary and the illocutionary act, as per the discussion in Section 4.2.2. However, as we will now see, its most common understanding in the field is actually tied to Searle's reappraisal of speech act theory rather than Austin's own original thinking (for a critical discussion, see Section 6).

Right from the start of a paper dedicated to Austin's locution/illocution distinction, Searle (1968: 405) stated: 'In attempting to explore Austin's notion of an illocutionary act I have found his corresponding notion of a locutionary act very unhelpful and have been forced to adopt a quite different distinction between illocutionary acts and propositional acts'. In his explanation for this move, Searle (1968: 407) posited that the locution/illocution distinction fails to be 'completely general, in the sense of marking off two mutually exclusive classes of acts' on the basis of the following rationale (inevitably simplified and adapted to fit the discussion up to this point):

- The locutionary act consists in producing an utterance with intelligible meaning.
- The presence of a performative verb in an explicit performative utterance cannot but be part of this meaning, which Austin attributes to locution.
- The function of the performative verb in such cases is to explicitly indicate the speech act's illocutionary force, which is something that belongs to the level of the illocution.
- It therefore follows that, at least in explicit performative utterances, the (purported) illocutionary act forms part of the locutionary act, when it should be independent from it.

Searle's solution to this apparent incongruity was to replace Austin's notion of the locution, as the more general act of saying something, with that of the *propositional act*, that is, the act of expressing the proposition encoded by the sentence that an utterance tokens in its production. Isolating the proposition – that is, just that part of the meaning of the uttered sentence that is truth-evaluable – allowed Searle to posit that any additional element that may be included in the utterance's form is simply an indicator of the utterance's force, and thus a determinant of the illocution. From this angle then, the problem that he had identified with locutionary acts largely evaporates, since 'the propositional act is not represented [...] by the entire sentence, but only by those portions of the sentence which do not include the indicators of illocutionary force', and 'so construed no propositional act is by itself an illocutionary act' (Searle, 1968: 421). In suggesting this,

Searle also provided a formula which seeks to capture the underlying form of the illocutionary act performed by explicit performative utterances, as follows:

$F(p)$

where the range of possible values for F will determine the range of illocutionary forces, and the p is a variable over the infinite range of possible propositions (Searle 1968: 420–421).

The appeal of Searle's proposal for the narrow view of pragmatics, and thus its associated role as a complement of semantic theory, should be fairly easy to appreciate. Separating the embedded (truth-evaluable) proposition from the performative matrix verb offers a principled way of accounting for the meaning of sentences that do not – at face value at least – fit the traditional truth-conditional approach. More specifically, in the case of an explicit performative, like '*I promise that I will come to your party.*', as in our familiar example in (6), we can still maintain that the uttered sentence does indeed carry some truth-evaluable content, in the sense of the proposition expressed by '*that I will come to your party*', without having to worry about the interference of the '*I promise*' part, which simply indicates the illocutionary force of a promise that this proposition is communicated with.

Within the same spirit, a concept that is central to Searle's reappraisal of speech act theory is that of an *illocutionary force indicating device* (henceforth IFID), which, if present in an utterance, can help determine the F in the aforementioned formula. In this respect, following Austin's original exploration of a grammatical criterion for performatives (see Section 4.1), Searle suggested that, apart from performative verbs (like '*promise*' in our example), IFIDs also comprise 'at least word order, stress, intonation contour, punctuation, [and] the mood of the verb' (1969: 30). By attributing this role to IFIDs, Searle's proposal became particularly popular for tackling a problem that semantic circles had traditionally characterised as central for any 'comprehensive theory of meaning for a natural language'; that is, the problem of 'all the sentences that seem not to have truth values at all: the imperatives, optatives, interrogatives, and a host more' (Davidson, 1967: 321). Effectively, Searle's formula allowed for an analysis of sentences in, say, the interrogative or the imperative, as in (34) and (35), by postulating that they express the same proposition as their corresponding declarative sentence, here offered in (33), with the distinct verb moods, word orders and intonation contours indicating each utterance's illocutionary force – that is, an assertion in (33),[12] a question in (34), and an order in (35).

---

[12] At this point, it is worth noting a further elaboration by Alston that is often presented in the relevant literature as an improvement on Searle's original take. According to Alston (1994),

33. *You will go to the school party on Friday.*
34. *Will you go to the school party on Friday?*
35. *Go to the school party on Friday!*

In this vein, even though it would eventually be argued that the postulation of a force marker for mood 'runs into difficulties' (Portner, 2004: 240), Searle's proposal was indeed instrumental for establishing that 'the semantics of the (major) morpho-syntactic sentence types – imperative, declarative and interrogative – determines the major illocutionary force types'; an assumption that still remains 'at the core of traditional speech act theory [...] and has [had] enormous impact on semantic-pragmatic theorising' (Ruytenbeek et al., 2017: 46).

5.2 Formal Updates to Speech Act Theory

Considering again the primacy that component pragmatics grants to semantics when it comes to the study of meaning, what probably cemented the popularity of Searle's elaborations on Austin's original theory was his continuous engagement with 'bringing formal order' to the description of speech acts (Culpeper & Haugh, 2014: 6; see also Section 6.1). Continuing – in essence – our discussion of Searle's contribution to the currently received view of speech act theory in pragmatics, we find his attempts to describe illocutionary acts with more analytical precision. In this regard, there are two more proposals of his which proved so successful in the field that they always accompany Austin's initial account in overviews of speech act theory– with one of them even demonstrably sidelining Austin's original position on the matter.

5.2.1 Felicity Conditions: From Regulative to Constitutive Rules

In the first instance, we encounter Searle's reappraisal of what Austin called conditions for the successful performance of a speech act (see Section 4.1.1). Searle's main proposal in this regard was that, on top of simply regulating the successful deployment of an illocutionary act, the relevant conditions can also be taken to effectively 'constitute' the act, in the sense of rendering its 'existence [...] logically dependent' on them (Searle, 1969: 34). By reassessing felicity conditions as *constitutive rules* of this sort, Searle returned to Austin's original list and reworked it into a set which aims at offering 'a model for explicating illocutionary acts in general' (Searle, 1969: 56) and thus comprises:

---

while the particular illocutionary force of the utterance of a declarative sentence is indeed determined in context, the form of the sentence itself restricts the range of illocutionary acts that it can be used to perform, determining thus its *illocutionary act potential*.

- the *propositional content condition*, which constrains the form of the utterance that embodies the illocutionary act under question;
- the *preparatory conditions*, which specify the preconditions for the illocutionary act's deployment;
- the *sincerity condition,* which stipulates the intention that the speaker needs to have in order to execute the illocutionary act; and
- the *essential condition*, which determines the illocutionary act's purpose.

Consider, for example, the illocutionary force of promising. Within this picture, an illocution counts as a promise if and only if it constitutes an undertaking on behalf of the speaker to do something (essential condition) that (a) the hearer would welcome and that (b) the speaker would not just normally do either way (preparatory conditions). Further, the act would need to refer to an undertaking that will take place in the future (propositional content condition) and which the speaker genuinely intends to follow through with (sincerity condition).

Apart from providing an alternative way of approaching illocutions, Searle's model was also designed with a view to allowing one to distinguish between them, by specifying the relevant conditions that underlie their differences. For instance, as we can see in Figure 2, this model enables us to determine that the difference between a request and an order is due to a specification of the social positioning of the speaker and the hearer, as stipulated by the extra preparatory condition in the case of the latter, which is included in its essential condition too.

		Request	*Order*
Types of rule	Propositional content	Future act A of H	Future act A of H
	Preparatory	1. H is able to do A. S believes that H is able to do A. 2. It is not obvious to either S or H that H will do A in the normal course of events out of their own accord.	1. H is able to do A. S believes that H is able to do A. 2. It is not obvious to either S or H that H will do A in the normal course of events out of their own accord. 3. S must be in a position of authority over H.
	Sincerity	S wants H to do A.	S wants H to do A.
	Essential	Counts as an attempt to get the H do A.	Counts as an attempt to get H to do A in virtue of the authority of S over H.

Key: H = hearer, S = speaker

Figure 2 Constitutive rules for requests and orders (after Searle, 1969: 66)

5.2.2 Searle's Taxonomy of Illocutionary Acts

Turning to another aspect of Searle's theoretical approach, which this time appears to have trumped Austin's initial exposition, we find his taxonomy of illocutionary acts. As evidenced by the extent to which it is not only simply referred to in the pragmatics literature, but also used to distinguish between different types of speech acts pretty much across the board in research in the field, Searle's reappraisal in this vein has been far more influential than Austin's original classification of illocutionary forces, which we encountered in Section 4.2.3. As we saw there, Austin's strategy was to group different kinds of performative verbs together on the basis of the illocutionary force that utterances embedding them are typically used to express. Again, much like with his proposal to replace locutionary with propositional acts, in his paper dedicated to this matter too, Searle (1975a: 345) starts his discussion by criticising this strategy:

> I shall try to keep a clear distinction between illocutionary verbs and illocutionary acts. Illocutions are a part of language as opposed to particular languages. Illocutionary verbs are always part of a particular language: French, German, English, or what-not. Differences in illocutionary verbs are a good guide but by no means a sure guide to differences in illocutionary acts.

Searle's counterproposal was to come up with a set of principles on the basis of which he would be able to distinguish between different illocutionary acts in a more systematic way and then construct his taxonomy accordingly.

To this end, he identified no less than twelve 'dimensions of variation' (Searle, 1975a: 345) in which illocutionary acts can be seen to differ from one another, even though his proposed classification ended up being based on mainly three of them; namely, differences in the act's illocutionary point, direction of fit and sincerity condition. The sincerity condition should sound familiar, since we have already encountered it in Searle's list of felicity conditions above. Then, even though this is not so transparent from its reworked name, the *illocutionary point* actually corresponds to the essential condition from the same list. In relation to this, Searle proposed this new label with a view to teasing apart distinct dimensions of what has so far been referred to as illocutionary force. His argument to this effect was that one can in principle distinguish between the actual purpose of an illocutionary act, that is, its illocutionary point, and the different features that specify the way in which this purpose is presented, with the illocutionary force being the superordinate term that includes both these aspects. Along these lines, a request and an order, as per their constitutive rules in Figure 2, can be conceived of as having the same illocutionary point (i.e., to get the hearer(s) to do something), but distinct illocutionary forces.[13] Turning to an illocutionary act's *direction of fit* now, this is actually linked to the act's propositional content and signifies the way in which the illocutionary force 'determines how that content is supposed to relate to the world' (Searle, 1975a: 347). In this regard, Searle distinguished between the words-to-world and world-to-words directions of fit, whereby the former characterises illocutions whose purpose is to provide a snapshot of a state of affairs in the world through their propositional content (hence the metaphorical allusion to the words fitting the world), while the latter relates to illocutionary acts whose purpose is to make their propositional contents a reality through their expression, or as this approach would have it, make the world fit the words.

On the basis of these criteria, Searle proposed a taxonomy of illocutionary acts, which comprises the five categories that have been summarised in Table 1.

In this taxonomy, we first encounter the category of *assertives* (or *representatives*), which, as the name suggests, are acts of asserting, in the sense of committing the speaker to the truth of their propositional content, as in (36).

36. *I have a pet dog.*

Seeing how they essentially pronounce the truth of a state of affairs, assertives constitute the only category in Searle's taxonomy with a words-to-world direction of fit, while their sincerity condition can be roughly equated to a belief, since their producers need to believe what they assert for their successful deployment.

Then, we have *directives*, which seek to get the hearer to do something, as in (37), and *commissives*, which conversely commit the speaker to doing something, as in (38).

37. *Close the window, please.*
38. *I will get you an expensive gift for your graduation.*

Both these types of illocutionary act exhibit a world-to-words direction of fit, since in both cases the propositional content does not represent an existing state of affairs, but is expressed with the purpose of bringing about a state of affairs (thereby making the relevant propositional content true) as a result of what the speaker wants the hearer to do in the first case, or what the speaker themself commits to doing in the second. By the same token, the relevant sincerity conditions are that of a genuine desire to get the hearer to do something and

---

[13] Among other overviews in the field, the term 'illocutionary point' is also preferred in this work's sister Element (Jucker, 2024). However, for ease of exposition, and especially since it is not uniformly used in most of the literature that I will be drawing from in my eventual argumentation, I have opted to not distinguish between illocutionary points and forces here.

Table 1 Searle's taxonomy of illocutionary acts

Category	Examples	Illocutionary point	Direction of fit	Sincerity condition
Assertives/ Representatives	*statements, descriptions, explanations, assertions, etc.*	Committing the speaker to something's being the case	Words-to-world	Belief
Directives	*requests, commands, questions, invitations, etc.*	Attempting to get the hearer to do something	World-to-words	Desire
Commissives	*promises, pledges, threats, guarantees, etc.*	Committing the speaker to some future course of action	World-to-words	Intention
Expressives	*apologies, congratulations, greetings, praises, etc.*	Expressing a psychological state about a state of affairs specified in the propositional content	N/a	Relevant psychological state
Declarations	*hirings, dismissals, wedding pronouncements, judicial orders, etc.*	Bringing about a correspondence between their propositional content and reality	Words-to-world AND World-to-words	N/a

a genuine intention on behalf of the speaker to follow through with their commitment, respectively.

Moving on to *expressives*, the illocutionary point is to express a psychological state, which the sincerity condition specifies and guarantees as genuine, in relation to the state of affairs that their propositional content describes. In this case, there is no direction of fit, since the truth of the propositional content is effectively presupposed. In (39), for instance, where the speaker rejoices at getting their license, they could not have expressed that they are happy about it, unless they had already got the license.

39. *I am so happy that I got my license!*

Finally, when it comes to *declarations*, exemplified next in (40), their defining characteristic is that they actually make their propositional content a reality by virtue of expressing it.

40. *I now pronounce you husband and wife.*

Interestingly, declarations have both directions of fit, as they do not just describe a state of affairs,[14] but effectively prescribe reality by making this state of affairs true through their deployment. Clearly, in this case, the sincerity conditions become immaterial, as the performance of a declaration is not so much a matter of the speaker being honest, as it is a matter of the speaker having the relevant authority to perform the declaration in the first place.

5.3 Illocutions as Acts of Speaker Meaning

While not directly related to it, Searle's taxonomy above can also help introduce yet another post-Austinian elaboration that has grown to take centre stage in the contemporary view of speech act theory in pragmatics. As already noted in Section 4.2.2, Austin conceived of illocutions as conventional acts. While discussing his notion of uptake there, we saw that, for an utterance of, say, '*Close the door!*' to constitute an order, there must be a convention linking the use of these words in this specific way with the issuance of an order. Obviously, the most straightforward way of appreciating this perspective is by considering prototypical examples of what Searle called declarations, as in (40), or, similarly, an utterance of '*I sentence you to 5 years in prison*', as in (9) quite further up.

Deferring the discussion of Austin's specific version of conventionalism to Section 6.2, it would be safe to say that his overall adherence to the

---

[14] Here, the state of affairs is obviously neither existing, as it is in the case of assertives, nor meant to become a reality in the future, as it is in the case of directives and commissives. It just becomes a reality as a result of the speech act itself.

conventionalist doctrine was met with a fair amount of contention by his peers from quite early on. Most famously, Strawson (1964) criticised Austin for focusing too much on ceremonial (almost institutionalised) speech acts, like the declarations just mentioned, and failing to see that his approach does not quite apply to the more basic illocutions that we casually perform in our everyday exchanges, and for which no relevant conventional procedure can be identified. To use an example of his own, consider the production of the utterance in (41) with a view to issuing a warning to a skater.

41. *The ice over there is very thin.*

As Strawson (1964: 444) pointed out, in cases like (41), it is highly unlikely that 'there is any statable convention at all [, ...] such that the speaker's act can be said to be an act done as conforming to that convention'. To address this issue, Strawson proposed a move away from Austin's conventionalism, which could of course be preserved when dealing with ritualised cases, and offered a reappraisal of Austin's account of the illocutionary act in intentionalist terms, using Grice's theory of meaning as his springboard. Obviously, at that point in time, Grice had not yet developed his theory of implicature, so Strawson's approach remained purely at the conceptual level of approaching illocutionary force as belonging to the remit of nonnatural *meaning*, or – as Grice preferred to refer to it – *meaning$_{NN}$*; that is, what we nowadays commonly refer to as speaker meaning.

As already noted in Section 2.1, Grice's 'Meaning' (1957) was the point of departure for a number of developments that would lead to the eventual recognition of speaker meaning as the remit of pragmatics for the narrow conception of the field. In this account, Grice (1957: 385) defined meaning$_{NN}$ as follows:

> *A* meant$_{NN}$ something by *x*" is (roughly) equivalent to "*A* intended the utterance of *x* to produce some effect in an audience by means of the recognition of this intention.

Even though this specific definition has been subject to numerous refinements through proposals that attempted to make its original exposition even more watertight,[15] I cannot dwell on it too much here due to space restrictions. In a nutshell though, through his postulation of meaning$_{NN}$, Grice is widely recognised to have worked out a more precise way of accounting for the intuition that 'communication is a matter of intentionally affecting another

---

[15] In fact, one such refinement was suggested by Strawson himself in the same paper discussed here, while another one can be found in Searle's *Speech Acts* too (1969: 42–50; see also Section 6.2).

person's psychological states' (Bach, 1999: 359). More specifically, he suggested that the way in which we get our interlocutors to understand what we intend to communicate to them is simply by getting them to recognise that we intend to communicate something to them in the first place.

Within this frame, Strawson (1964) argued that, notwithstanding the ceremonial cases that Austin had focused on, what he had referred to as 'the securing of uptake' can only be achieved if the audience recognises the speaker's relevant communicative intention. Therefore, since, as Austin insisted, this securing of uptake is a requirement for the successful performance of the illocutionary act, Strawson posited that the most reliable way of approaching the act itself would be by viewing it as *intentional*, and thus as part of meaning$_{NN}$.[16] In the years to follow, Strawson's suggestion gained significant traction, and 'speaker intention began to take the foreground in leading analyses of the illocutionary act' (Sbisà, 2022: 1312). Especially in the aftermath of the publication of 'Logic and Conversation' (Grice, 1975), and Searle's simultaneous introduction of the category of 'indirect speech acts', to which we will return shortly, it became increasingly commonplace for illocutionary acts like the one performed in the case of (41) to be approached as particularised conversational implicatures. From this angle, one would assume that the skater inferentially works out that the speaker uttered what they did with the intention of issuing a warning (to not skate at some particular spot), simply by following the cooperative principle and considering the utterance context.

The most influential, and perhaps also most systematic attempt to fully explicate this line of reasoning can be found in Bach and Harnish (1979). Like Strawson before them, Bach and Harnish recognised the existence of conventional illocutionary acts, but also suggested that the vast majority of illocutions are communicative in nature and thus need to be approached from an intention-based, inferentialist perspective. To this effect, they correspondingly posited that the success of these speech acts depends on the – by then – familiar Gricean process of pragmatic inference which is triggered by the hearer's recognition of the speaker's communicative intention. On this basis, they postulated a *speech act schema*, which constitutes a working out of the inference pattern that underlies the successful performance of speech acts. According to this schema, the hearer (a) recognises that the speaker is uttering

---

[16] Grice himself never engaged with the specific reappraisal of illocutionary force in terms of his theory of meaning – even though Levinson (2017: 205) does mention unpublished work of his dealing with the building up of complex speech acts on the basis of the mood of declarative, imperative and interrogative sentences. He was, however, particularly critical of the conventionalist approach (see, for example, Grice, 1989: Prolegomena), and also explicitly criticised Austin for ignoring 'the radical importance of distinguishing (to speak loosely) what *our* words say or imply from what *we* in uttering them imply' (Grice, 1986: 59; emphasis in original).

an expression, (b) accesses its operative meaning,[17] (c) understands what the speaker is saying (by engaging in reference assignment, disambiguation, etc.), and (d) infers the speaker's *illocutionary intention*. Obviously, in terms of the present discussion, the crux of this approach is this latter conception of an illocution as intentional action, which rests on salient contextual information (i.e., what Bach and Harnish called *mutual contextual beliefs*) and is regulated by the following uniformly applicable *communicative presumption* (Bach & Harnish, 1979: 7; emphasis my own):

> The mutual belief in CL[= the community of language users] that whenever a member *S* says something in [language] *L* to another member *H*, he is doing so with some *recognisable illocutionary intent*.

5.3.1 Indirect Speech Acts

Appreciating the challenge that cases of the sort that had concerned Strawson or Bach and Harnish pose for his own account too, Searle eventually also jumped on the speaker meaning bandwagon. Obviously, in the absence of any (explicit or implicit) IFIDs, warnings like (41) could not really fit his own formula for illocutionary acts, which we encountered in Section 5.1, either. To address this issue, Searle (1975b) introduced a distinction between *direct* and *indirect speech acts*, whereby the former would be reserved for utterances that exhibit a direct relationship between the type of sentence used and its utterance's illocutionary force and the latter would apply in cases of a corresponding mismatch, as in our familiar case in (41) when issued as a warning.

In this picture, Searle's take on (41) would be that its issuance as an assertion is effectively a *literal, secondary illocutionary act* by means of which the *primary illocutionary act* of warning is performed. Regarding the way in which this primary force is to be identified now, even though he did not use the term 'conversational implicature' per se, he did point to this very direction by suggesting that this process requires taking into account 'certain general principles of cooperative conversation (some of which have been discussed by Grice[18] [...]), and mutually shared factual background information of the speaker and the hearer, together with an ability on the part of the hearer to make inferences' (Searle, 1975b: 61). Against

---

[17] As Bach and Harnish (1979: 3) note, this expression is 'typically a sentence'. Effectively, by adding these two steps in the process, Bach and Harnish added an extra layer to Austin's tripartite description, by postulating the level of an *utterance act*, which is what triggers steps (a) and (b), before the locution – here (c) – and the illocution – here (d) – take over. In this way, this approach can be taken to address head on the criticism that Grice eventually launched against Austin, as per footnote 16.

[18] This was actually an explicit reference to Grice's 'Logic and Conversation' (1975) which was published in the same volume as Searle's paper under discussion here.

this backdrop, in Searle's updated approach, the way of accounting for the recognition – and thus uptake – of an indirect speech act's primary illocutionary force would follow the familiar Gricean route: the hearer first considers and rejects the explicit secondary illocution on the grounds that its felicity conditions do not apply in this case, and then pragmatically infers the implicit primary one against the context in which the utterance was produced.

At the same time, however, Searle also recognised that several indirect illocutionary acts appear to be performed by utterances which are still somehow 'conventionally used' to this effect (Searle, 1975b: 64). Using directives as his prototypical example, Searle identified no less than five different types of sentences that are ubiquitously used to indirectly perform this class of illocutionary acts, as exemplified in (42)–(46):

42. *Could you lend me some money?*
43. *Would you mind fetching me my phone from over there?*
44. *I would like to be alone now.*
45. *Are you going to wear this to school?*
46. *We'd all be better off if you stopped shouting.*

Clearly, it should not be that hard to think of specific contexts in which these declarative or interrogative sentences could be used as 'attempts to get the hearer to do something'; if anything, it might actually be harder to think of contexts in which they are not used as directives in the relevant sense. Still, their literal meaning relates to different aspects of what the speaker attempts to get the hearer to do in each case, rather than with actually getting the hearer to do it. For example, (42) concerns the hearer's ability, and (43) the hearer's willingness – or, in other cases, desire – to do what the speaker wants them to do. Along similar lines, (44) expresses a wish which is contingent on the hearer doing something, (45) focuses on the hearer's doing of something (that they should not), and (46) simply provides reasons for the hearer to do what the speaker wishes them to do. Notably, the relevant indirect acts can also be realised through various combinations of the above forms, as in (47):

47. *I hope it's not too much trouble if I ask if you could front me an advance on my paycheck this month.*

Regarding the reason why language users opt for indirect illocutions, when they could have easily gone with direct ones instead, Searle (1975b: 74) identified 'politeness' as 'the chief motivation – though not the only motivation – for using these indirect forms'.[19] Turning to his explanation for the apparent

---

[19] Needless to say, the intricate relationship between indirectness and politeness ended up taking centre stage in research on pragmatics too, especially after the independent recognition of politeness as

conventionality of certain indirect speech acts, this involved the addition to his account of an extra process of *conventionalisation*, whereby upon sufficient repetition of the same indirect primary illocutionary act by means of the same literal secondary illocution, the latter becomes an idiomatic form for the expression of the former. In line with Searle's idea, different proposals about how to theoretically approach such conventionalised indirect speech acts would treat them as either idioms (Sadock, 1974), in which case the identification of an indirect speech act's primary force would be attributed to a process of disambiguation that overrules the utterance's literal force without even considering it, or as *short-circuited implicatures* (Morgan, 1978), which are in principle calculable but not really calculated during interpretation.

5.4 Further Engagement with Speech Act Theory

Following the recognition of the category of indirect speech acts and the admittedly keen interest it generated, attention to speech act theory gradually started to fizzle out. As Levinson (2017: 201–202) notes in this vein, the 1980s witnessed an abundance of studies

> on indirect speech acts, investigating the forms used especially for requests across cultures, the psychological processing [...], and the politeness reasons for the mismatch between direct and indirect speech act coding. By the end of the 1980s, however, linguistic interests had moved largely elsewhere.

As Kissine (2012: 169) correspondingly asserts, in recent years, 'the main contemporary pragmatic theories of utterance interpretation devote little space, if any at all, to the way utterances are interpreted as speech acts, that is to the way they are assigned an illocutionary force'. When talking about utterance interpretation here, Kissine alludes of course to the so-called cognitive turn in pragmatics, which started dominating the field in the 1990s by shifting the focus from the mainly philosophical discussion of speaker meaning to the investigation of the inferential processing that underlies its recovery during verbal communication. Still, within this setting too, most of the work that has specifically touched on speech act theory over the past forty years or so has, for the most part, remained consonant with the received view outlined in this section.

A notable exception to this can be found in the case of relevance theory, the proponents of which famously argued that 'the vast range of data that speech-act theorists have been concerned with is of no special interest to pragmatics' (Sperber

---

a core area in the field (for a detailed overview, see Culpeper & Terkourafi, 2017). As is well-known, indirect speech acts feature prominently in the original rationale behind both Brown and Levinson's (1987) politeness theory and Leech's (1983) exposition of his tact maxim, that is, two works that, alongside Lakoff (1973), were the first to put politeness on the pragmatics map.

& Wilson, 1995: 243). In a nutshell, the rationale behind this position is that, since speech acts are in their essence mainly social or institutional, illocutionary force assignment is not a necessary part of utterance comprehension; that is, hearers do not always need to recognise – let alone (meta)represent – the force with which an utterance was produced in order to work out its intended meaning. Rather, the extent to which this assignment is needed depends on whether the interpretation of an utterance requires such an attribution to achieve relevance, in the sense of yielding enough worthwhile information to offset the cognitive effort that the hearer spends in the process.[20] In this picture, there are only three generic speech acts whose mental representation is deemed essential for the comprehension process, namely those of 'saying', 'asking', and 'telling'. Recall, for instance, our examples in (33)–(35) – repeated in the following as (48)–(50) for convenience.

48. *You will go to the school party on Friday.*
49. *Will you go to the school party on Friday?*
50. *Go to the school party on Friday!*

For relevance theorists, the mood indicators of an utterance's underlying sentence belong to a wider category of linguistically encoded semantic constraints, dubbed *procedures* (after Blakemore 1987; see also Wilson & Sperber, 1993), which are specifically designed to guide the inferential comprehension process to some particular interpretive outcome. On this occasion, the relevant procedure would be to lead the hearer to embed the speaker's explicitly expressed proposition in a higher-order speech act description. Assuming that our examples mentioned previously are addressed by, say, Mary to George, the descriptions for (49) and (50) could be approximated as in (51) and (52), respectively.

51. Mary is asking George whether he will go to the school party on Friday.
52. Mary is telling George to go to the school party on Friday.

From a relevance-theoretic angle then, (51) would be approached as a mental representation that describes a desirable thought, in the sense of marking Mary's expectation for a relevant answer, while (52) as one that describes a desirable state of affairs.[21]

Notwithstanding the extent to which illocutionary force attribution may be compulsory during utterance interpretation, it would appear at first sight that relevance theory's approach to sentence mood may have something in common

---

[20] Due to space restrictions, I cannot go into the specifics of relevance theory, including its technical notion of the property of relevance, here. I therefore defer the reader to one of the numerous overviews of it in the literature (e.g., Wilson & Sperber, 2004; Assimakopoulos, 2017). For the relevance-theoretic discussion of speech acts specifically, see Sperber and Wilson (1995: 243–254).

[21] For more details, including the relevance-theoretic distinction of descriptive and interpretive use on which this account is based, see Wilson & Sperber (1988).

with Searle's position presented in Section 5.1, since, in both cases, the proposition expressed by the declarative sentence in (48), when this sentence is transformed into an interrogative or imperative form in (49) and (50), continues to be embedded in the corresponding speech act representation. This conclusion, however, would be incorrect. Contrary to the Searlean picture, where, as we have seen, illocutionary forces are *determined* by the semantics of sentence types, in relevance theory they are *always* '*recovered by a mixture of decoding and inference* based on a variety of linguistic and non-linguistic clues' (Wilson & Sperber, 2004: 623; emphasis my own). As one may have guessed by now, reference is made here to the broader literalism/contextualism debate (see, e.g., Recanati, 2004b) that has dominated (narrow) pragmatics over the past couple of decades. For relevance theory, which falls under the contextualist camp, it is not only the illocutionary force carried by an utterance of an interrogative or imperative sentence, but even the very basic proposition explicitly expressed by the declarative form that requires contextual input.[22] For Searle, on the other hand, illocutionary forces can, in principle at least, be traced at the semantic level too, since, as per his *principle of expressibility*, 'whenever one wishes to make an utterance with force F, it is always possible to utter a sentence the meaning of which expresses exactly force F' (Searle, 1968: 418).[23]

Despite the importance of the literalism/contextualism debate for modern pragmatic theory, neither the relevance-theoretic approach outlined earlier nor the overall debate itself is featured in recent pragmatically oriented overviews of speech act theory. All in all, it would seem that, at least as far as pragmatics is concerned, research on speech act theory has indeed reached a standstill. Given the centrality of the topic for the discipline though, this is rather astonishing, especially considering that 'contemporary literature is rife with confusions' in relation to 'illocutionary force attribution' (Kissine, 2012: 170) as well as that 'the most fundamental issues' surrounding speech acts have also not been 'resolved at all' (Levinson, 2017: 200). As we will now turn to see though, perhaps things are not as grim as they sound at this point.

---

[22] That is because relevance theory endorses the linguistic underdeterminacy thesis, according to which, 'linguistically encoded meaning *never* fully determines the intended proposition expressed' (Carston, 2002: 49; emphasis in original) and thus an utterance's semantic content 'always needs considerable contextual input to gain full propositional status' (Assimakopoulos, 2008: 107). Given the need of this input, and on par with 'implicature', the proposition explicitly expressed by an utterance is dubbed *explicature* in this picture. By association then, when this arises in interpretation, its combination with an illocutionary force is correspondingly dubbed a *higher-order* explicature.

[23] While it is certainly tempting to associate Searle with the literalist camp, it is widely accepted that his 'philosophy of language contains a notorious tension between a literalist view on the relationship between sentences and their meanings, and what [...] appears to be a virulent defence of contextualism' (Kissine, 2011: 115).

6 Back to the Origins: An Evaluation of the Received View

In contrast to the picture painted just now, in his sister Element, Jucker (2024: 4–5) offers an alternative explanation for the current state of research on speech acts, attributing its perceived standstill to 'the context of a move away from philosophical methods and introspection to more empirical methods', as follows:

> The 1980s saw a growing interest in the newly emerging field of pragmatics [...]. This was a time when linguistics was still dominated by formalist approaches that focused on linguistic structures and analytical tools that relied on native speaker intuition and invented sentences that were used as the basis for theorising. Against this background, pragmaticists began to ask questions about actual language usage. Speech acts were no longer seen as abstract entities that could be dissected with philosophical rigour into a set of constitutive felicity conditions. Instead, they came to be seen as performance phenomena whose realisation could be investigated across different groups of speakers. (Jucker, 2024: 4)

At that, if the wealth of empirical studies surveyed in Jucker's Element is any indication, it is hardly the case that pragmatic research on speech acts simply 'went out of fashion' (Levinson, 2017: 200); rather, it is the interest in speech act theory that would appear to have taken a back seat in recent years. In fact, this empirical turn appears to have even revealed a new profile for speech acts, enabling pragmaticists to view them as

> *fuzzy* entities whose function is often *negotiated in context* [...]. The focus, therefore, shifts from the speaker who performs a certain speech act to the interaction between two or more speakers. The illocutionary [force] of a speech act *emerges* in the interaction and depends on *the degree of conventionalisation* of a specific speech act and the way it is (implicitly or explicitly) interpreted by the interlocutor(s). (Jucker, 2024: 5; emphasis my own)

Obviously, this outlook is largely at odds with the picture presented in Section 5, which in turn begs the question of why the conceptual core of speech act theory, at least as it is presented in most textbooks or handbooks on pragmatics, has not yet aligned itself with it.

As I will argue in this section, the apparent stagnation of speech act theory is not coincidental. It rather has to do with the firm grip that the narrow conception of the field has for long had on pragmatic theory, inevitably affecting the way in which pragmaticists theorise about speech acts too. In an early paper of his, Levinson (1979: 390) aptly summarised the received view's most common 'way of thinking about the properties that individuate different illocutionary forces', as a process of 'factor[ing] out the set of necessary and sufficient conditions for the non-defective performance of the relevant speech act'. In this picture, speech act theorists have traditionally 'tended to see their job as dismantling the hybrid theory of speech acts and parcelling out the felicity conditions to either the semantic or pragmatic component where they are thought more properly to belong' (Levinson, 1979: 392); hence, for example, the attribution of an utterance's force to its underlying sentence's (explicit or implicit) IFIDs in the case of direct speech acts and to the inferential recognition of the speaker's intentions in that of indirect ones within the dominant Searlean tradition. Obviously, looking at speech acts as 'fuzzy entities negotiated in context' would be particularly problematic in this setting, since, as Levinson (1979: 392) correspondingly put it, 'if felicity conditions are variable in relation to discourse context, then none of them are the sort of thing one wants in an orderly semantics in any case'.

So, ironically enough, it seems that our overview of the contemporary landscape has led us back to pretty much the same thing that motivated the original exposition of speech-act theory in the first place; that is, Austin's postulation of the descriptive fallacy as an entrenched, but conceptually incomplete and somewhat compromised approach to the study of linguistic meaning. As I will now turn to discuss, the parallels with the corresponding evolution of pragmatic theory over the past fifty years or so are quite striking.

6.1 On Meaning

Going back to Section 2, we can recall that during its establishment as a discipline in its own right, pragmatics was predominantly conceptualised, on par with the component view, as an 'add-on' to traditional semantic theory – the latter being itself an offshoot of the same 'ideal language philosophy' tradition that was responsible for the advent of logical positivism around Austin's time. By the 1960s logical positivism had of course collapsed; yet, the scholarly fascination with formal analysis lived on. On the premise of the famous Montagovian argument that 'there is [...] no important theoretical difference between natural languages and the artificial languages of logicians' (Montague, 1974: 222), the 1970s witnessed the inception of formal semantics, which admittedly dominates linguistic thought to this very day. Ever since, truth conditions, compositionality and the general discussion of propositional content have remained at the centre of attention, as the main, if not exclusive foci of semantic investigation. This time though, those aspects of meaning that could not fit into formal theory were no longer perceived as deficiencies of natural language that render sentences meaningless – perhaps a result of the earlier demise of logical positivism. Instead, they were to be systematically investigated within the purview of (component) pragmatics.

From this angle, it was clear that Austin had made a valid point about the challenges that performatives pose for formal accounts of linguistic meaning, which he solidified further by showing that even constatives behave in the same way; the key challenge being that the meaning of utterances formulated as explicit performatives cannot really be assigned a truth value. Given this, and considering also the discussion in Section 5.1, it should be safe to assume that a main reason why Searle's account 'proved attractive to linguists' (Levinson, 2017: 201) was that, by replacing Austin's locutionary acts with propositional acts, it offered a principled way of tackling this very issue, while also safeguarding the purity of the formal approach through the reintroduction of propositional contents in the equation.

Going back to Austin's original work, however, it is clear that the very notion of a speech act was developed with a view to altogether criticising, rather than endorsing, the traditional understanding of meaning in terms of propositions and truth conditions. For instance, while recapping his overall discussion in his final lecture, Austin (1975: 148; emphasis my own) stated that 'the need for the general theory [of speech acts] arises simply because the traditional "statement" [i.e., the object of enquiry for traditional truth-conditional accounts of meaning] is an abstraction, an ideal, and *so is its traditional truth or falsity*'. Then, right after that, while listing some 'morals' of his account, he additionally stipulated that

> truth and falsity are (except by an *artificial abstraction* which is always possible and legitimate for certain purposes) *not* names for relations, qualities, or what not, but for a dimension of assessment – how the words stand in respect of satisfactoriness of the facts, events, situations, etc., to which they refer [... and, therefore,] the familiar contrast of 'normative or evaluative' as opposed to the factual is *in need* [...] *of elimination*. (Austin, 1975: 149; emphasis my own)

On top of this, Austin had previously even questioned the extent to which truth or falsity themselves are objective measures. More specifically, during his already mentioned 'objective assessment of the accomplished utterance', Austin (1975: 143) reached the conclusion that 'in real life, as opposed to the situations envisaged in logical theory, one cannot always answer in a simple manner whether [a constative ...] is true or false'. From this angle, as Sadock (2004: 57) aptly puts it, truth and falsity are in a way best seen as a convenient shorthand for assessing a specific group of illocutions: 'with illocutionary acts of assertion, statement, and the like, we happen to call correspondence with the facts *truth* and a lack of it *falsity*, whereas in the case of other kinds of illocutions, we do not use those particular words'.

Of course, the issue here is not whether Searle's proposal to substitute locutionary acts with propositional ones was somehow internally incoherent; after all, it provided an elegant alternative to Austin's original notion of the locution, which apparently resonated better with scholars in the field. It is rather that 'the introduction of propositions into Austin's account of speech acts is not only not needed, but also inconsistent with the general picture of speech that Austin intend[ed] to provide' (Sbisà, 2024: 258). To make matters worse, Searle's proposal has somehow managed to trump Austin's original take to such an extent that, in the collective conscience of pragmaticists today, it is taken to be essentially co-extensive with what Austin himself had in mind when postulating speech acts in the first place. In other words, as Oishi (2016: 337) points out, it is nowadays 'taken for granted that Austin's seminal idea of speech acts is developed and completed by Searle, in spite of the fact that their ideas are different at crucial points'. As a result, overviews of speech-act theory, including those found in the pragmatics literature, use the term 'locutionary act' to describe what is in essence Searle's propositional act. On top of this, they also substitute – pretty much without fail – Austin's explicit reference to 'meaning' (in juxtaposition to 'force') with reference to 'content'. Consider, for example, the following formulation by Harris et al. (2018: 22; emphasis my own) in their very recent overview of the contemporary speech-act-theoretic landscape:

> For Austin and Searle, these are distinctions between two levels of abstraction at which we may individuate speech acts. *A locutionary or propositional act* is a speech act individuated only in respect of its *content*, and illocutionary force is the extra ingredient bridging the gap from sense and reference to the full illocutionary act.

To be fair of course, Austin was not particularly forthcoming about his actual views on what meaning amounts to. The admittedly few scattered comments that he made in relation to his use of the term in *How to Do Things with Words* were rather cryptic, equating meaning with the traditional conceptions of sense and reference, which he took 'on the strength of current views' (Austin, 1975: 149). However, he did explicitly state that the 'notion of correspondence with facts' which pertains to locutions needs to be 'over-simplified because essentially it brings in the illocutionary aspect' (Austin, 1975: 146) and additionally recognised that 'the theory of "meaning" as equivalent to "sense and reference" will certainly require some weeding-out and reformulating in terms of the distinction between locutionary and illocutionary acts' (Austin, 1975: 149).[24] What is more, upon consideration of Austin's collective works, one can readily see that, apart from being 'critical of the identification of meaning with truth-conditions', he also 'rejected the objectification of "meanings"' (Sbisà, 2012: 5). All in all, as Sbisà (2012: 12) points out, for Austin, 'meaning is [...] something dynamic, something people do, and it is misleading to deal with it as with an entity or object' (Sbisà, 2012: 12).[25] Ultimately though, this is precisely what Searle's proposal to substitute the locutionary with the propositional act brought back into the picture, by essentially suggesting that 'there must be something – the proposition: mental object, abstract object or whatever it may be – corresponding to the sentence uttered so as to constitute its meaning' (Sbisà, 2012: 13).

Perhaps more crucially even, the Searlean tradition did not just stop there. It objectified illocutionary force too, treating it as a 'component of meaning' (Searle & Vanderveken, 1985: 7) and eventually incorporating it in logical analysis even, by suggesting that 'the ideal language of a universal grammar [à la Montague] must contain logical constants and operators capable of generating names for all possible illocutionary forces of utterances' (Searle & Vanderveken, 1985: 7–8).[26] In a way, as Burkhardt (1990: 125) pointed out around the time that pragmatic interest in speech-act theory had already started to dwindle, it seems that, as time went by, 'speech act theorists, in one way or other, ha[d] put the cart before the horse and [...], slowly, the insight began to grow that linguistic action is much more a (lexical) semantic than a pragmatic problem'.[27] No wonder then that, by the 1990s, the relationship of pragmatics with speech act theory had already started to weaken, with pragmatic interest shifting to the study of speech acts as 'performance phenomena' that exhibit variation across 'different groups of people'.

---

[24] If anything, statements of this sort appear to suggest that Austin perhaps foresaw the criticism that, as we saw in Section 5.1, Searle would eventually launch in this vein.

[25] For an extensive discussion of Austin's conception of truth and meaning, see Sbisà (2024: Part 4).

[26] In fact, a highly influential parallel trajectory can be encountered in the syntactic study of speech acts too, following Ross's (1970: 223) famous postulation of the *performative hypothesis*, according to which, 'declarative sentences [...] must be analysed as being implicit performatives, and must be derived from deep structures containing an explicitly represented performative main verb'. Interestingly, even though pragmaticists have suggested that 'the performative hypothesis has long been abandoned' (Huang, 2014: 124), research on it is actually still going strong (see, for example, Wiltschko, 2021).

[27] Notably, this is a development that Burkhardt (1990: 125) actually welcomed, since his explicit aim in the relevant paper was to 'accelerate the movement already prevailing in speech act philosophy by putting the semantic horse before the pragmatic cart again'.

6.2 On Intention

To my mind, a parallel argument can also be made in relation to the role that the (equally entrenched) Gricean conception of speaker meaning has played in pragmatically oriented appraisals of speech act theory. Again, of course, the issue is not whether intention-based accounts of speech acts are somehow ill-formed in their inherent argumentation, but rather that they specifically cater to completing the received view's formally oriented description of speech acts, departing again in substantial ways from Austin's original rationale. In relation to this latter point, Sbisà's (2009: 35) observation in the following is certainly telling:

> Given the well-known divergences between Austin and Grice with respect to several philosophical problems [...], it should be clear from the very beginning that any project aiming to make sense of Austin in a Gricean framework, however valuable from a theoretical point of view, could not lead to a reliable clarification of Austin's own views and might therefore miss some essential feature of the notions he wanted to introduce.

As we have already seen, intention-based approaches to illocutionary force are largely attributed to Strawson, with Bach and Harnish playing a key role in their solidification. However, Searle also interfered with their contemporary conceptualisation, albeit more indirectly. Recall, from Section 5.3, Grice's definition of meaning$_{NN}$, reproduced next for convenience:

> "A meant$_{NN}$ something by x" is (roughly) equivalent to "A intended the utterance of x to produce some effect in an audience by means of the recognition of this intention.

Upon formulating this definition, Grice (1957: 385) further noted that 'to ask what A meant is to ask for a specification of the intended effect (though, of course, it may not always be possible to get a straight answer involving a "that" clause, for example, "a belief that ... ")'. Considering Grice's exemplification of this intended effect in terms of a belief and seeing how that belief would ultimately be the hearer's, in speech-act-theoretic terms, it would follow that, for Grice, what we are dealing with is essentially a perlocutionary effect. Recognising this, Searle (1969: 47) famously argued that the said effect should be conceived of as illocutionary instead, since it 'consists simply in the hearer understanding the utterance of the speaker' rather than 'a belief or response'.

Now, it is widely accepted that Searle's reappraisal of speech acts in terms of constitutive rules (see Section 5.2.1) was intended to align, even if weakly so, his theoretical exposition with Austin's conventionalism; the relevant hypothesis being that 'the semantic structure of a language may be regarded as a *conventional* realization of a series of sets of underlying constitutive rules, and [...] speech acts are acts characteristically performed by uttering expressions in accordance with these sets of constitutive rules' (Searle, 1969: 37; emphasis my own). Still, by semanticising[28] illocutionary force in this way while additionally suggesting that the illocutionary effect consists in the hearer 'simply understanding' the speaker's meaning, Searle (like Strawson) can be seen to have directly contributed to 'an impoverishment of the heuristic potential of the notion of illocutionary act in the analysis of verbal interaction' (Sbisà, 2009: 37).

In order to fully appreciate the relevant argument, we need to briefly circle back to the original Austinian notion of *illocutionary effect*. As already mentioned in Section 4.2.2, for Austin, illocutionary effects comprise the securing of uptake and the recognition of the typical effects that a speech act customarily brings about. Since the securing of uptake amounts to the securing of 'the understanding of the meaning and of the force of the locution' in this picture, if one is prepared to overlook the (significant of course) divergence in the contemporary received view with respect to the Austinian locution, some sort of equivalence could be established. What we are still missing, however, are 'the typical effects a speech act customarily brings about'; that is, the two extra categories of illocutionary effects that Austin (1975: 117) identified: (a) the 'certain ways' in which 'the illocutionary act "takes effect"' and (b) the invitation 'by convention of a response or sequel' by some illocutions. Considering these in turn, we can readily witness an interesting picture emerging.

Unfortunately, as Sbisà (2009: 44) points out, the passage through which Austin introduced the 'taking effect' of the illocutionary act is 'rather mysterious' and the example he used to this effect is 'not a very helpful one', since it refers to a highly ceremonial act, which could easily be categorised as 'conventional' by an intentionalist:

> The illocutionary act 'takes effect' in certain ways, as distinguished from producing consequences in the sense of bringing about states of affairs in the 'normal' way, i.e. changes in the natural course of events. Thus, 'I name this ship the *Queen Elizabeth*' has the effect of naming or christening the ship; then certain subsequent acts such as referring to it as the *Generalissimo Stalin* will be out of order. (Austin, 1975: 117)

---

[28] On the basis of our discussion so far, one could justifiably conclude that illocutionary forces do not really fit in the study of semantics, as they make no contribution to the truth-conditional content of the proposition expressed by an utterance. Assuming, however, that semantics is also concerned with conventional, 'timeless meaning' à la Grice (1957), the study of IFIDs, which belong to the 'expressions' in Searle's quotation right above, could very well still be attributed to it, as the relevant devices conventionally point to specific illocutionary forces.

Still, Sbisà offers an astute argument about how Austin's insight on this occasion can (and probably should) be extended to cover all kinds of illocutions. Based on a juxtaposition with natural causation, which would be the 'normal' way of bringing about consequences (that is, perlocutionary effects in this context), Sbisà (2009: 45) suggests that illocutionary effects arise due to 'changes in states of affairs belonging to the same level of reality as norms', which in turn belong to 'the realm of social conventions'. From this angle, understanding the speaker's utterance as having a particular illocutionary force means taking it as an invocation of a socially determined procedure with a recognisable effect. So, in Austin's example mentioned just now, and insofar as there are no infelicities in the performance of the illocutionary act at hand, we take the ship to have a new name *because* we understand the speaker's utterance as belonging to the recognisable procedure of naming a ship. By the same token, alluding back to Strawson's example in (41), in the absence of infelicities, we take it that the speaker 'should not be attributed responsibility for whatever may happen to us in connection with the warning's content', *because* 'we understand that the speaker's utterance has the force of a warning' (Sbisà, 2009: 49). From this angle, if we are to posit, as Austin would, that these effects are conventional rather than intentional, their uptake would be secured through (tacit or explicit) intersubjective agreement, which also safeguards that they can be annuled in the presence of infelicities in the speech act's deployment (on this point, see Sbisà, 2007). Viewed in this way, the securing of uptake can be decoupled from speaker intentions, as an illocutionary act's 'taking effect' would be the result of both the speaker and the hearer agreeing on the speech act's illocutionary force.

To a large extent, this approach is additionally supported by the third kind of illocutionary effect posited by Austin, that is, the 'invitation of a response or sequel'. While this specific effect only applies to some speech acts, like questions (which invite answers) or offers (which invite an acceptance or refusal), it can still be taken to indicate that, at least in these cases, 'to perform an illocutionary act means to initiate a reproduction of an interaction pattern[29] that involves the speaker's utterance and the hearer's cooperative response to it' (Witek, 2015: 43). Obviously, the illocutionary effect in this case consists in the invitation of the sequel, with the sequel itself – i.e., the answer, the acceptance or refusal – being a perlocutionary effect; yet, a consideration of the latter can in

---

[29] The use of the term 'interactional pattern' here refers specifically to Millikan's (2005) biological model of language, which I take, however, to be co-extensive with a 'blueprint' for illocutionary effects, in the broader sense discussed in Section 7.1 (for a critique though, see Sbisà, 2024: 48–52).

principle also be deemed essential for the attribution of an illocutionary force to the speech act. As Sbisà (1992: 101–102) discusses, that is because,

> if the hearer's uptake is necessary for the carrying out of an illocutionary act, in order to know whether a certain illocutionary act has been carried out we should first know whether an uptake has been achieved. And this we can know from a consideration of the response (verbal or non-verbal) which follows the illocutionary act under examination, since each response makes manifest how the hearer has taken the speaker's illocutionary act. It seems therefore that, when we want to assign a definite illocutionary force to a certain speech act, we should take the hearer's response into account.

In order to see how speech act theory could accommodate this angle, the following argument by van Rees (1992: 40; emphasis in original) can be particularly illuminating:

> Illocutionary acts involve the attainment of a *communicative* effect by producing verbal utterances with the intention of getting a listener to recognize, by recognizing that one has that intention, what particular attitude (belief, want, intention, affect) with respect to a particular state of affairs one is trying to express. Perlocutionary acts involve the attainment of an *interactional* effect by trying to bring about further effects on the cognitive, affective, or conative state of the listener by way of the communicative act. One and the same utterance is used to perform both communicative and interactional acts,[30] the one being a conventional means for the achievement of the other.

Despite having been made in the context of the criticism that speech-act theory cannot adequately account for ordinary conversation, launched against it by conversation analysts this time, van Rees' argument can be seen to further substantiate Sbisà's emphasis on the hearer's response. However, the relevant nuance of Austin's original account that is being referred to on both these occasions has been pushed to the background in the contemporary received view. That is because right from the beginning of his engagement with speech act theory, Searle (1969: 23; emphasis my own) has consistently referred to '*complete* speech acts as asserting, questioning, commanding, etc.', using 'the name "*illocutionary acts*"'; a practice that has now been adopted by most speech act theorists, who use the labels 'speech act' and 'illocutionary act' interchangeably.

Going back to his original argumentation though, it is pretty clear that Austin would never endorse an equivalence of the total speech act with the illocution alone, since in his model the 'introduction of illocution between locution and perlocution prevents any conflation between meaning on the one hand, and

---

[30] The nomenclature here is due to van Eemeren and Grootendorst (1984).

efficacy in arousing feelings, dispositions, and reactions on the other' (Sbisà, 2024: 57).[31] In this regard, Austin's explicit aim in the second half of his lecture series may have been to 'fasten on the illocutionary act', but his reason for doing so, as we also saw in Section 4.2.2, was because he wanted to 'contrast it with the locutionary and perlocutionary ones', rather than give it exclusive priority. As Oishi (2016: 337) further explains, for Austin,

> the concepts of the locutionary, illocutionary and perlocutionary acts [we]re invented for elucidating different sources and effects of language use, not for confining speech acts in real life by classifying them into rigid classes. This essence of Austin's speech act theory is hardly recognised, which is largely due to the identification of Austin's theory with Searle's.

Indeed, from early on in *How to Do Things with Words* and while talking about constatives even (that is, utterances that were either way considered meaningful because of their truth conditions), Austin (1975: 52; emphasis my own) asserted that

> to explain what can go wrong with statements [=constatives] *we cannot just concentrate on the proposition involved* (whatever that is) as has been done traditionally. *We must consider the total situation in which the utterance is issued* – the total speech-act.

This is something that he insisted on with respect to all speech acts, as he notably reiterated this position in his already mentioned final 'morals' too, where he emphasised that 'the total speech act in the total speech situation is the *only actual phenomenon* which [...] we are engaged in elucidating' (Austin, 1975: 148; emphasis in original).

6.3 Speech Act Theory and the Scope of Pragmatics

Considering that the motivation behind its original exposition was a need to show that the analysis of linguistic utterances goes far beyond the formal descriptive dimension, it is truly remarkable how, during its evolution, speech act theory ended up getting highly formalised too. As discussed in this section, this can be straightforwardly attributed to the domination of component pragmatics as the main conceptualisation of the field over a number of decades. After all, when one is to treat pragmatics as an add-on to semantic theory, what better way to incorporate speech acts within its remit than by grounding them on a semantic basis (through the postulation of the propositional act and accompanying IFIDs) and then attributing any extra meaning that they may carry over and above this basis (as in cases of indirection) to the tried and tested Gricean paradigm.

---

[31] I need to thank an anonymous reviewer for drawing my attention to this observation.

As a result, however, the pragmatic essence of speech acts has been severely impoverished, to the extent that current pragmatic theorising no longer engages with speech act theory, at least as much as its centrality for the discipline should be prompting it to. Within this frame, the recognition of illocutionary force has been reduced to a mainly categorical exercise, with forces themselves having been stripped of much of their role as functions of actions that bring about conventional effects of a varied (social, interpersonal, conversational ...) nature. At the same time, the parallel focus on speaker intentions has rendered perlocution irrelevant for pragmatic enquiry, since by 'stop[ping] so to speak at the recognition by the hearer of the illocutionary intentions of the speaker' the question of 'whether the hearer believes an assertion, executes an order, complies with a request, etc is not a subject of pragmatic rules' (van Dijk, 1977: 199). Clearly, all this has played a pivotal role in the attested diminishing interest in speech act theory, whereby 'after the initial enthusiasm of the 1970s, so many scholars doing research on verbal interaction turned to other approaches' (Sbisà, 2009: 37).

Against this backdrop, if we are to identify the main reason why the theoretical discussion of speech acts within pragmatics has taken a back seat in recent years, we may well point again to Burkhardt's (1990: 125) metaphorical reference to 'the decline' of the paradigm:

> in the course of [...] its history, speech act theory has undergone a development from the Austinian pragmatic beginnings via different, more or less intentionalist approaches and Searle's 'hybrid' conception to what might be called a (lexical) semantic view of speech acts. Here, I think, speech act theory has come to an end.

7 Speech Acts as Context-Driven Actions

Despite the aforementioned diminishing interest, as we saw in Section 6, empirical research in pragmatics has still revealed a new profile for speech acts, which, however, differs substantially from the picture presented in Section 5. In relation to this, combining the discussion so far with the juxtaposition of narrow and broad pragmatics presented in Section 2 can give us further insight about where the relevant difference of perspective comes from, and how it could perhaps be mitigated.

In his already mentioned textbook on *Pragmatics* and while considering what I have here called the 'received view' of speech act theory, Levinson (1983: 263–276) observed that all pragmatic accounts of speech acts to date had to at least accept some version of what he dubbed the *literal force hypothesis*, that is, the underlying assumption that the illocutionary force of an utterance needs to be built into (if not be even determined by) its base sentence. From the point of view of component pragmatics, this is hardly surprising, since, as we saw in Section 2.3, the starting point for the narrow conception of the field is linguistic representation itself. A direct repercussion of this hypothesis though, as Levinson also points out, is that, in all cases of indirect speech acts, the secondary, literal force of the utterance under question needs, in the very least, to be traceable during the derivation of the indirect primary illocutionary force.

Indeed, considering the discussion in Section 5.3.1, this is something that applies across the board when it comes to the received view of speech act theory. For Searle's account, for example, an indirect illocution's primary force may be worked out via Gricean pragmatic inference, but this can only happen after the literal illocutionary force is rejected in the first place. Similarly, for accounts opting for a treatment of indirect speech acts in idiomatic terms, the primary illocutionary force would need to be selected among options that should in principle also include the secondary, literal illocutionary force; otherwise, we would not be able to distinguish between an utterance of (53) as an indirect request during a dinner party and its utterance as a direct ability-related question posed by a doctor while a patient is trying out a new prosthetic hand.

53. *'Can you pick up that fork?'*

According to Levinson (1983: 264), since at least for some kinds of speech acts, such as requests, the vast majority of usages is indirect, with empirical evidence additionally indicating that 'the kinds of sentences that are thus employed are very varied', the literal force hypothesis essentially gets trivialised: 'on the face of it, what people *do* with sentences seems quite unrestricted by the surface form (i.e. sentence-type) of the sentences uttered' (Levinson, 1983: 265; emphasis in original). Crucially, as Levinson further remarks, this calls into question our entire hypothesis, since, by eliminating the need to posit a literal secondary illocution, there is no longer a need to call the indirect act primary anymore; it is essentially the only illocutionary act performed by the production of the relevant utterance. If anything, this opens up the way for a reconceptualisation of speech act theory, whereby illocutionary force is mapped directly 'onto sentences in context', and thus becomes 'entirely pragmatic' (Levinson, 1983: 274).

Even though this is not specifically commented on in his argumentation, it should be evident from the discussion so far how Levinson's rationale could be taken to challenge the traditional treatment of speech acts from the narrow pragmatic angle. By accepting that 'illocutionary force [...] has no direct and simple correlation with sentence-form or -meaning' (Levinson, 1983: 274), its identification no longer needs to start from an examination of its underlying utterance's linguistic representation. At the same time, in line with the top-down approach adopted by broad pragmatics, the realisation that this force could actually be 'mapped directly onto sentences in context' would render the contextual conditions that allow this mapping to take place as the point of departure for the study of speech acts. Following this rationale, this section will concentrate on how such a perspective, which, as we saw in Section 2.3, views contexts as being determined by 'the interlocutors' patterns of interaction' and 'the conditions of society', can be incorporated in our theoretical understanding of speech acts. At that, considering Austin's insistence that a theory of speech acts should be concerned with 'the total speech act in the total speech situation', chances are that he may have in principle also welcomed such a possibility – or at the very least, it is highly unlikely that he would have excluded any aspect of the phenomenon simply because it does not conform to some ideal of formal order or intentionalism.

7.1 Operationalising Context

In order to understand the role that context can be taken to play in the delineation of speech acts from the broad pragmatic angle, we need to first appreciate how, in this conception, it goes beyond the description of a mere frame within which utterances are situated. For perspective pragmatics, contexts of verbal interaction additionally comprise sets of affordances that enable verbal exchanges to unravel in specific ways through the coordinated actions of the interlocutors. Echoing to some extent Levinson's independent idea of a direct mapping of illocutionary force onto sentences in context, Mey (2001: 228; emphasis my own) correspondingly notes that, for broad pragmatics, speech acts[32]

> are pragmatic because they base themselves on language *as constrained by the situation*, not as defined by syntactic rules or by semantic selections and conceptual restrictions [...]; in the final analysis, they are determined by the broader social context in which they happen, and they realize their goals in the conditions placed upon human action by that context.

Anyone familiar with the relevant literature should recognise the literature should recognise this description as directly linked to Mey's notion of the *pragmeme* as a 'general situational prototype, capable of being executed in

---

[32] As is well-known, in his account, Mey (2001) actually readdressed the remit of traditional speech act theory and replaced the very concept of a speech act with that of a *pragmatic act*, which is also what he referred to on this occasion specifically. However, in the interest of avoiding giving the impression that what we are dealing with here pertains to a different concept than that of a speech act, as originally envisaged by Austin, I have opted to not take on Mey's term of choice in the present discussion.

the situation' (Mey, 2001: 221). Since for Mey (2001: 228) pragmemes 'correspond pretty closely to what Levinson, in an earlier article, ha[d] called "activity types"', however, for the purposes of the present exposition, I will treat these two terms as co-extensive. To elucidate the relevant notion, let's look at the exchange in (54) between a customer *C* and a shopkeeper *S* in the rather familiar context of a short visit to the grocery shop:

54.   *S (to last customer):* Bub-bye.
      C: Some apples please. Just help myself is that alright?
      S: Yes they're all fine.
      C: Yes they look good.
      S: // // There, that's eighteen, orright?
      C: uhuh. You've just got the one kind of lettuce?
      S: Yes. Cos.
→ *C:* That's a nice one.
      S: Yes. They are getting proper now aren't they. Thirty six please.
      // // thank you very much.
      C: Thanks. Goodbye.

(Levinson, 1979: 372)

Now, consider *C*'s utterance of '*That's a nice one*', which was presumably produced while pointing to some specific lettuce in this setting. As Levinson (1979: 372; emphasis in original) points out, on this particular occasion, this single utterance simultaneously '*counted as* selecting a lettuce, requesting that it be wrapped, and undertaking to pay for it', since 'there were no further negotiations about the lettuce' later on, and all these three actions were eventually fulfilled.[33] This example effectively shows that, being first and foremost social (rather than simply linguistic) actions, speech acts also rely heavily on the discourse context in which they are situated. What activity types, or indeed pragmemes, add to the picture then is a set of affordances or 'strict constraints on contributions to any particular activity' which give rise to 'strong expectations about the functions that any utterances at a certain point in the proceedings can be fulfilling' (Levinson, 1979: 377). For Levinson (1979: 371; emphasis in original), these affordances constitute '*inferential schemata* [..., which] are tied to [...] the structural properties of the activity in question', but regardless of the way in

---

[33] Incidentally, the present discussion also shows how straightforwardly an account of speech acts as context-driven actions can deal with the challenge of *illocutionary pluralism*, whereby 'a speaker perform[s] many different speech acts, which are all on a par and all of which are addressed to the very same hearer' (Lewiński, 2021a: 6698), while also predicting that such occurrences arise quite naturally in mundane conversation.

which we may approach their specific logical or cognitive instantiation, the upshot is that they ultimately mediate verbal behaviour.

From the point of view of the present discussion, such an appraisal would suggest that the relevant contextual information is not just responsible for working out non-literal illocutionary forces, as per the received view on speech act theory, or for determining whether and how illocutionary force assignment is part of the process that leads to the reconstruction of speaker meaning, as a contextualist alternative, like the relevance-theoretic one presented in Section 5.4 might suggest. Discourse context is rather part and parcel of the way in which interlocutors coordinate their verbal exchanges, for it ultimately provides them with *blueprints of the typical procedures for – and effects of – particular speech acts*; a position that I take to be fully consonant with Austin's conventionalism, as presented in Section 6.2.

7.2 Speech Acts in Interaction

Remaining on the discussion in Section 6.2, recall also how the interactional angle should also feature centrally in our theory of speech acts. Obviously, as already seen in Section 2.2, broad pragmatics is well-equipped to handle this, since it either way views meaning-making as an essentially collaborative process, whereby all interlocutors '*co-construct* meanings on the fly through tacit negotiations that take place as their interaction unravels'. In this respect, looking at instances of mundane conversation suggests that this may well apply to the identification of a speech act's illocutionary force too.

Consider, for instance, the exchange in (55) which also took place in our familiar setting of a casual visit to the grocery shop:

55.   *C:* Do you have pecan Danish today ?
    → *S:* Yes we do. Would you like one of those ?
        C: Yes please
        S: Okay ((turns to get))
                            (Merritt, 1976: 324; as cited in Levinson, 1983: 359)

Note *S*'s first turn in the transcript above. It starts with an utterance that is a direct answer to *C*'s question in the previous turn and then continues with the issuance of an indirect act of offering. In the course of the overall interaction, however, it is fairly clear that *S*'s performance of the speech act of offering is actually prompted by the question in *C*'s original turn. Exemplifying the role of the discourse context as a blueprint for typical exchanges in specific settings, the adoption of the interactional perspective allows us to explain how *C*'s seemingly information-seeking question is additionally interpreted by *S* as carrying the force of a request on this occasion.

As Levinson (1983: 356–364) famously showed in his reanalysis of indirect requests, focusing on the position of a particular utterance in the course of an exchange can offer an alternative understanding of the way in which illocutionary forces are assigned to utterances during verbal interaction. Obviously, in order to appreciate this alternative, it is essential to first get briefly acquainted with some key terms in the conversation-analytic tradition (for a complete overview, see Levinson, 1983: Chapter 6). The main ingredients that we will need for this are the notions of 'preference organisation', 'adjacency pair', and 'pre-sequence', as well as the analytical term 'position'. Starting with the latter, given that mundane conversation is typically a matter of continuous turn-taking, the term *position* is used in this setting to refer to the place of a turn, which typically plays some specific function in relation to other turns within an organised conversational sequence. For example, in the case of a question-answer *adjacency pair*, which we actually encountered twice in (55), the presence of a question in position 1 is typically expected to be followed by an answer in position 2. *Preference organisation* now has to do more specifically with the way in which such conversational sequences are customarily organised in the interest of promoting social solidarity. In the case of making a request, for instance, the *preferred* (that is, the unmarked) next turn would be one of granting the request, with a rejection being *dispreferred* (i.e., marked) in the relevant structural sense. Finally, in this setting, *pre-sequences* are turns that initiate a particular conversational move with a view to prefiguring a preferred next turn.

Within this frame, Levinson's reanalysis attributed to indirect requests the role of a pre-sequence, as follows. From a conversation-analytic viewpoint, a prototypical request sequence exhibits a four-position structure, as in the case of (56), which again takes place in our familiar context.

56. Position 1 – *C:* Hi. Do you have uh size C flashlight batteries ?
 ((PRE-REQUEST))
 Position 2 – *S:* Yes sir ((GO AHEAD))
 Position 3 – *C:* I'll have four please ((REQUEST))
 Position 4 – *S:* ((turns to get)) ((RESPONSE))
 (Merritt, 1976: 324; as cited in Levinson, 1983: 357)

Since, in terms of social solidarity, the dispreferred response in the case of a request is that of a refusal, the typical inclusion of a pre-request in the sequence is meant to check for the most likely grounds for such a refusal, with the presence of such grounds effectively allowing the initiator of the request to abort it altogether, as we can observe in (57):

57. → C: Do you have Marlboros ?
    → S: Uh, no. We ran out
    C: Okay. Thanks anyway
    S: Sorry
                           (Merritt, 1976: 325; as cited in Levinson, 1983: 358)

Still, as we already saw in (55), on top of offering grounds for refusal, pre-requests also allow the recipient to change the entire sequence from one of requesting to one of offering. That is because, for conversation analysts, in the presence of 'preferences between alternative sequence types, and therefore between alternative first parts of adjacency pairs [...], a pre-sequence can elicit from its recipient the preferred first part', which suggests that, since 'offers [a]re structurally preferred to requests as a way of getting transfers accomplished [, ...] a pre-request can get an offer next, obviating the need for actually doing the request' (Schegloff, 1979: 49). This much can even happen directly, as exemplified in (58):

58.   C: Have you got Embassy Gold please ?
     S: Yes dear ((provides))
                           (Sinclair, 1976: 60; as cited in Levinson, 1983: 361)

Following this rationale, Levinson concluded that, when it comes to the structural organisation of requests in verbal interaction – on condition, of course, that these are not aborted, as in (57) – there is a quite marked preference ranking: The most preferred sequence is one that directly goes from a position-1 pre-request to a position-4 response, as in (58), followed by a sequence where the pre-request prompts an offer on the part of the interlocutor, as in (55), with the otherwise prototypical sequence where the pre-request is followed by an invitation to make the request overtly, as in (56), being least preferred in this vein.

Regardless of the actual validity of this analysis of indirect requests as pre-requests (see, e.g., Fox, 2015), what it quite clearly problematises is the traditional assumption that a speech act is tied exclusively to its producer's choice of expression (for direct speech acts) or intention (for indirect ones). In this regard, the adoption of a conversation-analytic perspective can offer a fresh look that conforms with the view of speech acts as context-driven actions, in the sense discussed in Section 7.1. That is because it offers a principled way of identifying whether uptake has been secured through its so-called *next-turn proof procedure*, whereby 'the display of [the parties' understandings of prior turns' talk] in the talk of subsequent turns affords both a resource for the analysis of prior turns and a proof procedure for professional analyses of prior turns – resources intrinsic to the data themselves' (Sacks et al., 1974: 729).

At the same time, the relevance of the conversation-analytic method for the broad pragmatic perspective should be self-evident too. After all, as Bilmes (1988: 161–162; emphasis my own) underlines, conversation analysis provides a model

> that is neither statistical *nor intentional*-motivational. Instead, the analysis is *structural*, done by reference to contextual features, especially *sequencing*, and to *conventional understandings and procedures*. It looks for mechanisms that produce and explain behaviour, but for *social* rather than psychic mechanisms. Its concern is with relevance, intelligibility, and systemic function. [In this picture, rules are thus viewed ...] as *conventional reference points that actors orient to and that give behaviour its particular intelligibility.*

Circling back to the discussion in Section 6.2 then, it seems that this approach can be very usefully implemented in the accommodation of the interactional angle within speech act theory in a way that additionally aligns well with Austin's purported conventionalism. This is something that Levinson (2017: 204) also underlines, when he notes that, since 'for success, the action depends on the uptake' the extent to which 'almost all speech acts are joint actions' is 'a fundamental aspect of speech acts neglected in Searlian analysis'.

7.3 Speech Acts and the Conditions of Society

Having further motivated the conceptualisation of speech acts as 'sequentially positioned and contextually sensitive' (Deppermann & Haugh, 2022: 3), we can now turn to the way in which the conditions of society could also feature in a revamped theoretical account of speech acts that embraces the broad view of pragmatics. The main line of argumentation in this vein should be intuitively straightforward: since the execution of speech acts depends on the blueprints of typical procedures and effects that the discourse context engenders, and these blueprints are either way socially determined, speech acts are by default conditioned by society too.

For example, there is by now overwhelming evidence that 'different cultures find expression in different systems of speech acts, and that different speech acts become entrenched, and, to some extent, codified in different languages' (Wierzbicka, 1985: 146). Clearly, this is why risks can arise in performing even the simplest speech act in the context of intercultural communication. Mey (2016: 122–123) offers a pertinent example:

> In Japan [...] one cannot just approach a random passer-by on the streets and perform a simple speech act of 'requesting information' (like '*Where is the nearest sushi-bar?*'), as one would do in one's Western home country.

> Like any other action, such a Japanese request should be prefaced by a 'preparatory' act, intended to unlock the common space in which any social interaction in Japan has to take place. In practice, this means that one first has to ask for permission to invade the other person's privacy [...]. Failure to observe this pragmatic pre-condition on any 'public' speech acting will prevent one from getting across to one's addressee [...] (Mey, 2016: 122–123)

Technically speaking, what we are dealing with in this case is a request that is not completed due to a hitch in its deployment (see Section 4.1.1). Clearly, what causes the hitch is the difference in the conventional procedure of performing a request in the speaker's own culture vis-à-vis the Japanese one, which hinders and thus blocks the securing of uptake and, by extension, the intended perlocutionary effect from being realised. The limitation of the received view of speech act theory in this vein should also be evident: focusing solely on the intentions of the speaker may indeed allow us to recognise the speech act as a request, but its apparent misexecution remains unaccounted for, unless we allow for the relevant sociocultural considerations to enter the picture.

To be completely fair, the social dimension is of course not entirely alien to the received view of speech act theory. For instance, as we saw in Section 5.2.1, Searle distinguished between requests and orders on the grounds of the social positioning of the speaker and the hearer. What is more, he has also acknowledged that a 'sentence only determines a set of truth conditions (or other sorts of conditions of satisfaction) against a background of assumptions and practices' (Searle, 1980: 231), many of which are clearly social. Even so, this acknowledgment came with the caveat that we cannot really explicate these assumptions and practices 'without generating an infinite regress' (Searle, 1983: 148). Therefore, as Pratt (1986: 60) has noted, 'while often acknowledging the[ir] theory's dependence on undeveloped assumptions about social interaction, [speech act philosophers] argue that it is impossible to develop these assumptions in any satisfactory way'.

Pratt's illuminating discussion in that very same paper reveals yet another shortcoming of the received view of speech acts, which this time applies to the component pragmatics tradition as a whole.

> Like most contemporary linguistics, speech-act theory implicitly adopts one-to-one speech as the norm or unmarked case for language use. Examples and descriptions of speech acts always refer to *the* speaker and *the* hearer, and questions of intention and inference are always formulated in terms of only these two presences. (Pratt, 1986: 61; emphasis in original)

Indeed, one-to-one exchanges may be generally taken as prototypical within the domain of verbal interaction, but in reality they represent a rather idealised scenario. As Pratt (1986: 61) rightly points out, several verbal exchanges involve 'multiple participants with multiple intentions toward one another', while at the same time 'people have myriad encounters each day with utterances directed at a mass addressee' too – an angle that has undoubtedly become particularly relevant with the advent of traditional and more recently social media as well. Making a similar observation, albeit in the context of discussing argumentation this time, Lewiński (2021b: 435) remarks that 'this seemingly innocuous fact has the potential to turn speech act theory on its head', since 'the whole communicative transaction – the speaker's complex intention [...] and the hearers' uptake – cannot be described anymore as a dyadic affair'. Obviously, this is something that the narrow take on pragmatics, with its focus on one-to-one exchanges, cannot straightforwardly address. Broad pragmatics, on the other hand, offers a perspective that naturally lends itself to analysing verbal interaction of a more complex nature, since, by starting from the discourse context, it considers 'pragmatic acting [of any sort...] as adapting oneself, linguistically and otherwise, to one's world [...] and within the affordances it puts at [one's] disposal' (Mey, 2001: 215). In this picture then, a pragmatic analysis of speech acts in polylogues would begin from a consideration of the discourse context in which they take place (e.g. a party game, a political debate, social media, etc.) and its specific affordances.

Finally, on top of the characteristics of the social setting in which the (dialogical or polylogical) interaction takes place, there is a further sense in which linguistic action is fundamentally influenced by the conditions of society. As Pratt (1986: 68) has again aptly put it, the received view of speech act theory has largely overlooked the fact that 'people always speak from and in a socially constituted position, a position that is, moreover, constantly shifting, and defined in a speech situation by the intersection of many different forces'. As one might be able to deduce from this quotation, reference is made here to the more general study of discursive practice as mediated by ideology.

Following Langton's (1993) analysis of pornography as an illocutionary act of subordination and silencing towards women and Altman's (1993) appraisal of hate speech as an illocutionary act of treating someone as a moral subordinate, there is by now a rich literature applying speech act theory to the investigation of social issues underpinned, among other things, by the use of language in specific ways. Notably though, a common characteristic of all these approaches is that they base their argumentation mainly on Austin's original exposition, and specifically on the distinction between illocution and perlocution, rather than on the further elaborations that formed the received view presented in Section 5 (which, as we saw in Section 6.2, also pushed perlocution to the side). In fact, in one of the more recent papers following this trend, Saul (2018: 361) recognises that the mainstream conception of speech act theory still has limitations when it comes to discussing ideologically-charged language use, as in the case of political manipulation through dogwhistling:[34]

> These new discussions have not yet moved far enough away from the focus on content. Fully making sense of politically manipulative speech will require a detailed engagement with certain forms of speech that function in a less conscious manner – with something other than semantically expressed or pragmatically conveyed content ...

Indeed, as the prolific research within the domain of Critical Discourse Studies has famously revealed, discourse is both 'socially constitutive', and 'socially conditioned' (Fairclough & Wodak, 1997: 258), in the sense that 'it does not only influence, but also reflects [...] social practices' (Assimakopoulos, 2021b: 397). From our present perspective, this realisation alone should grant society a theoretical role that is much deeper than simply that of distinguishing between particular speech acts like requests and orders. Again, as Mey (2001: 320; emphasis in original) has correspondingly argued, the perspective take on pragmatics can accommodate this angle too:

> Different language use is not just a matter of linguistic variation, to be described and classified in purely theoretical terms, or to be analyzed with the aid of sociological variables denoting class or other societal parameters. The main impact of pragmatics as a *social* science is in the ways it helps us to recognize social discrimination and motivates us to work toward ending it.

8 By Way of Conclusion

With our overall discussion drawing to a close, it is worth recalling Jucker's (2024) depiction of a speech act within the contemporary pragmatics landscape. If what we are dealing with are indeed fuzzy entities of varying degrees of conventionalisation, whose illocutionary forces emerge as a result of (tacit) interactional negotiation in context, it is clear that their theoretical treatment from the point of view of narrow pragmatics can only go so far. That is because, from this new angle, the attribution of illocutionary force is no longer unduly dependent on an utterance's underlying sentence form, its propositional content or the speaker's intentions in producing it. In contrast, the broad take on the

---

[34] Dogwhistling consists in the practice of using suggestive language that will be recognised only by some members of an audience, thus avoiding critical scrutiny by everyone else, and is approached by Saul as a covert perlocutionary act – covert in the sense that 'it does not succeed if the intended perlocutionary effect is recognized as intended' (Saul, 2018: 377). For a comparable discussion of illegal hate speech as an overt perlocutionary act, see Assimakopoulos (2020).

scope of pragmatics can easily accommodate this alternative understanding of speech acts, since it does not only acknowledge more factors that play a role in the speech act's issuance or identification, but additionally posits that it is ultimately the discourse context which drives this process, by projecting particular functions that utterances may fulfil at various stages of a verbal exchange. In this picture, both sociocultural and interactional considerations can be seen to play a central role, as they often underlie differences in the discourse context's projections. So, as already foreseen by Haberland and May (see Section 2.3), when it comes to theorising about speech acts, the focus could indeed shift from the meaning of their underlying utterances to the conditions that govern their production, with the main overarching question becoming: *'Why has this utterance been produced?'*

Interestingly, this is something that was anticipated by Levinson (1983: 278) quite some time ago, when he suggested that there are 'some compelling reasons to think that speech act theory may slowly be superseded by much more complex multi-faceted pragmatic approaches to the functions that utterances perform'. Clearly, the aim of the present Element has been to motivate rather than present such an account, by problematising the primacy that has been granted to the formal, intentionalist appraisal of a concept whose original exposition was specifically designed to resist such a treatment. Given the entrenched nature of traditional speech act theory, any attempt at revision is of course likely to face considerable resistance; yet, such an update may not only further unlock our understanding of speech as action, but also reveal new ways of systematising pragmatic theory. After all, empirical research in the field has already superseded the traditional narrow conceptualisation of speech acts. Perhaps it is time for our theoretical outlook on them to get updated too, in a way that is bound to align better with Austin's original aim of explaining 'the total speech act in the total speech situation.'

References

Alston, William P. 1994. Illocutionary acts and linguistic meaning. In Savas L. Tsohatzidis (ed.) *Foundations of Speech Act Theory: Philosophical and Linguistic Perspectives*. London: Routledge, pp. 29–49.

Altman, Andrew. 1993. Liberalism and campus hate speech: A philosophical examination. *Ethics* 103(2): 302–317.

Ariel, Mira. 2010. *Defining Pragmatics*. Cambridge: Cambridge University Press.

Assimakopoulos, Stavros. 2008. Intention, common ground and the availability of semantic content: A relevance-theoretic perspective. In Istvan Kecskes & Jacob L. Mey (eds.) *Intention, Common Ground and the Egocentric Speaker-Hearer*. Berlin: de Gruyter Mouton, pp. 105–126.

Assimakopoulos, Stavros. 2017. Relevance. In Anne Barron, Yueguo Gu & Gerard Steen (eds.) *The Routledge Handbook of Pragmatics*. London: Routledge, pp. 310–322.

Assimakopoulos, Stavros. 2020. Incitement to discriminatory hatred, illocution and perlocution. *Pragmatics and Society* 11(2): 177–195.

Assimakopoulos, Stavros. 2021a. Beyond meaning$_{NN}$ and ostension: Pragmatic inference in the wild. In Elly Ifantidou, Louis de Saussure & Tim Wharton (eds.) *Beyond Meaning*. Amsterdam: John Benjamins, pp. 11–28.

Assimakopoulos, Stavros. 2021b. Interpretation, relevance and the ideological effects of discursive practice. *Pragmatics & Cognition* 28(2): 394–415.

Assimakopoulos, Stavros. 2022. Ostension and the communicative function of natural language. *Journal of Pragmatics* 191: 46–54.

Austin, John L. 1953. How to talk: Some simple ways. *Proceedings of the Aristotelian Society, New Series* 53(1952–1953): 227–246.

Austin, John L. 1962. *How to Do Things with Words* (edited by James Opie Urmson). Oxford: Oxford University Press.

Austin, John L. 1975. *How to Do Things with Words*, 2nd ed. (edited by James Opie Urmson and Marina Sbisà). Cambridge, MA: Harvard University Press.

Ayer, Alfred Jules. 1936. *Language, Truth, and Logic*. London: V. Gollancz Ltd.

Bach, Kent. 1999. Grice, H. Paul. In Robert A. Wilson & Frank C. Keil (eds.) *The MIT Encyclopedia of the Cognitive Sciences*. Cambridge, MA: MIT Press, pp. 359–360.

Bach, Kent. 2012. Context dependence. In Manuel García-Carpintero & Max Kölbel (eds.) *The Continuum Companion to the Philosophy of Language*. London: Continuum, pp. 153–184.

Bach, Kent & Robert M. Harnish. 1979. *Linguistic Communication and Speech Acts*. Cambridge, MA: MIT Press.

Bar-Hillel, Yehoshua. 1971. Out of the pragmatic wastebasket. *Linguistic Inquiry* 2(3): 401–407.

Bilmes, Jack. 1988. The concept of preference in conversation analysis. *Language in Society* 17(2): 161–181.

Blakemore, Diane. 1987. *Semantic Constraints on Relevance*. Oxford: Blackwell.

Blakemore, Diane. 1992. *Understanding Utterances*. Oxford: Blackwell.

Brown, Penelope & Stephen C. Levinson. 1987. *Politeness: Some Universals in Language Usage*. Cambridge: Cambridge University Press.

Bublitz, Wolfram & Neal R. Norrick. 2011. Introduction: The burgeoning field of pragmatics. In Wolfram Bublitz & Neal R. Norrick (eds.) *Foundations of Pragmatics*. Berlin: de Gruyter Mouton, pp. 1–20.

Burkhardt, Armin. 1990. Speech act theory – the decline of a paradigm. In Armin Burkhardt (ed.) *Speech Acts, Meaning and Intentions: Critical Approaches to the Philosophy of John R. Searle*. Berlin: Walter de Gruyter, pp. 91–128.

Carston, Robyn. 2002. *Thoughts and Utterances: The Pragmatics of Explicit Communication*. Oxford: Blackwell.

Chapman, Siobhan. 2006. *Thinking about Language: Theories of English*. Basingstoke: Palgrave Macmillan.

Culpeper, Jonathan. 2021. Sociopragmatics: Roots and definition. In Michael Haugh, Dániel Z. Kádár & Marina Terkourafi (eds). *The Cambridge Handbook of Sociopragmatics*. Cambridge: Cambridge University Press, pp. 15–29.

Culpeper, Jonathan & Michael Haugh. 2014. *Pragmatics and the English Language*. Basingstoke: Macmillan.

Culpeper, Jonathan & Marina Terkourafi. 2017. Pragmatic approaches (im)politeness. In Jonathan Culpeper, Michael Haugh & Dániel Kádár (eds.) *The Palgrave Handbook of Linguistic (Im)politeness*, 11–39. Basingstoke: Palgrave Macmillan.

Davidson, Donald. 1967. Truth and meaning. *Synthese* 17(3): 304–323

Davis, Steven. 1991. Introduction. In Steven Davis (ed.) *Pragmatics: A Reader*, 11–39. Oxford: Oxford University Press.

Deppermann, Arnulf & Michael Haugh. 2022. Action ascription in social interaction. In Arnulf Deppermann & Michael Haugh (eds.) *Action Ascription in Interaction*. Cambridge: Cambridge University Press, pp. 3–27.

van Dijk, Teun A. 1977. *Text and Context: Explorations in the Semantics and Pragmatics of Discourse*. London: Longman.

van Eemeren, Frans H. & Rob Grootendorst. 1984. *Speech Acts in Argumentative Discussions*. Berlin: De Gruyter Mouton.

Elder, Chi-Hé. 2024. *Pragmatic Inference*. Cambridge: Cambridge University Press.

Fairclough, Norman & Ruth Wodak. 1997. Critical discourse analysis. In Teun van Dijk (ed.) *Discourse Studies: A Multidisciplinary Introduction (Vol. 2): Discourse as Social Interaction*. London: Sage, pp. 258–284.

Fox, Barbara. 2015. On the notion of pre-request. *Discourse Studies* 17(1): 41–63.

Garcés-Conejos Blitvich, Pilar & Maria Sifianou. 2019. (Im)politeness and discursive pragmatics. *Journal of Pragmatics* 145: 91–101.

Garcés-Conejos Blitvich, Pilar. 2024. *Pragmatics, (Im)Politeness, and Intergroup Communication*. Cambridge: Cambridge University Press.

Green, Mitchell S. 2021. Speech acts. In Edward N. Zalta (ed.) *The Stanford Encyclopedia of Philosophy* (Fall 2021 ed.), https://plato.stanford.edu/archives/fall2021/entries/speech-acts/.

Grice, H. Paul. 1975. Logic and conversation. In Peter Cole & Jerry L. Morgan (eds.) *Syntax and Semantics, Vol. 3: Speech Acts*. New York: Academic Press, pp. 41–58. Reprinted in Grice, 1989, pp. 22–40.

Grice H. Paul. 1957. Meaning. *The Philosophical Review* 66(3): 377–388. Reprinted in Grice, 1989, pp. 213–23.

Grice, H. Paul. 1986. Reply to Richards. In Richard E. Grandy & Richard Warner (eds.) *Philosophical Grounds of Rationality*. Oxford: Clarendon, pp. 45–106.

Grice, H. Paul. 1989. *Studies in the Way of Words*. Cambridge, MA: Harvard University Press.

Haaparanta, Leila. 2013. Philosophy and its recent history: Remarks on *What is Analytic Philosophy?* by Hans-Johann Glock. *Journal for the History of Analytical Philosophy* 2(2): 2–5.

Haberland, Hartmut & Jacob L. Mey. 1977. Editorial: Linguistics and pragmatics. *Journal of Pragmatics* 1(1): 1–12.

Haberland, Hartmut & Jacob L. Mey. 2002. Linguistics and pragmatics, 25 years after. *Journal of Pragmatics* 34(12): 1671–1682.

Harris, Daniel W. Daniel Fogal & Matt Moss. 2018. Speech acts: The contemporary theoretical landscape. In Daniel Fogal, Daniel W. Harris & Matt Moss (eds.) *New Work on Speech Acts*. Oxford: Oxford University Press, pp. 1–39.

Haugh, Michael. 2008. Intention in pragmatics. *Intercultural Pragmatics* 5(2): 99–110.

Horn, Laurence R. 2004. Implicature. In Laurence R. Horn & Gregory Ward (eds.) *The Handbook of Pragmatics*. Oxford: Blackwell, pp. 3–28.

House Juliane & Dániel Z. Kádár. 2021. *Cross-Cultural Pragmatics*. Cambridge: Cambridge University Press.

Huang, Yan. 2010. Anglo-American and European Continental traditions. In Louise Cummings (ed.) *The Pragmatics Encyclopedia*. London: Routledge, pp. 13–15.

Huang, Yan. 2014. *Pragmatics*, 2nd ed. Oxford: Oxford University Press.

Jucker, Andreas. 2024. *Speech Acts: Discursive, Multimodal, Diachronic*. Cambridge: Cambridge University Press.

Katz, Jerrold J. 1977. *Propositional Structure and Illocutionary Force: A Study of the Contribution of Sentence Meaning to Speech Acts*. Cambridge, MA: Harvard University Press.

Kecskes, Istvan. 2010. The paradox of communication: Socio-cognitive approach to pragmatics. *Pragmatics and Society* 1(1): 50–73.

Kecskes, Istvan. 2014. *Intercultural Pragmatics*. Oxford: Oxford University Press.

Kissine, Mikhail. 2011. Misleading appearances: Searle on assertion and meaning. *Erkenntnis* 74(1): 115–129.

Kissine, Mikhail. 2012. Sentences, utterances, and speech acts. In Keith Allan & Kasia M. Jaszczolt (eds.) *The Cambridge Handbook of Pragmatics*. Cambridge: Cambridge University Press. pp. 169–190.

Lakoff, Robin. 1973. The logic of politeness: Or, minding your *p*'s and *q*'s. In *Proceedings from the Annual Meeting of the Chicago Linguistic Society* (Volume 9, Number 1), pp. 292–305.

Langton, Rae. 1993. Speech acts and unspeakable acts. *Philosophy & Public Affairs* 22(4): 293–330.

Leech, Geoffrey N. 1983. *Principles of Pragmatics*. London: Longman.

Levinson, Stephen C. 1979. Activity types and language. *Linguistics* 17(5–6): 365–400.

Levinson, Stephen C. 1983. *Pragmatics*. Cambridge: Cambridge University Press.

Levinson, Stephen. C. 2017. Speech acts. In Yan Huang (ed.) *The Oxford Handbook of Pragmatics*. Oxford: Oxford University Press, pp. 199–216.

Lewiński, Marcin. 2021a. Illocutionary pluralism. *Synthese* 199: 6687–6714.

Lewiński, Marcin. 2021b. Speech act pluralism in argumentative polylogues. *Informal Logic* 41(3): 421–451.

Linell, Per. 1998. *Approaching Dialogue: Talk, Interaction and Contexts in Dialogical Perspectives*. Amsterdam: John Benjamins.

Merritt, Marilyn. 1976. On questions following questions in service encounters. *Language in Society* 5(3): 315–357.

Mey, Jacob L. 2001. *Pragmatics: An Introduction*, 2nd ed. Oxford: Blackwell.

Mey, Jacob L. 2016. Pragmatics seen through the prism of society. In Keith Allan, Alessandro Capone & Istvan Kecskes (eds.) *Pragmemes and Theories of Language Use*. Cham: Springer, pp. 105–132.

Mey, Jacob L. & Mary Talbot. 1988. Computation and the soul. *Journal of Pragmatics* 12(5–6): 743–789.

Millikan, Ruth Garrett. 2005. *Language: A Biological Model*. Oxford: Oxford University Press.

Montague, Richard. 1974. *Formal Philosophy: Selected Papers of Richard Montague* (edited by Richmond H. Thomason). New Haven: Yale University Press.

Morgan, Jerry L. 1978. Two types of convention in indirect speech acts. In Peter Cole (ed.) *Syntax and Semantics, Vol. 9: Pragmatics*. New York: Academic Press, pp. 261–280.

Morris, Charles. 1938. Foundations of the theory of signs. In Otto Neumeth, Rudolf Carnap & Charles Morris (eds.) *International Encyclopedia of Unified Science*. Chicago: University of Chicago Press, pp. 77–138.

Oishi, Etsuko. 2016. Austin's speech acts and Mey's pragmemes. In Keith Allan, Alessandro Capone & Istvan Kecskes (eds.) *Pragmemes and Theories of Language Use*. Cham: Springer, pp. 335–350.

Portner, Paul. 2004. The semantics of imperatives within a theory of clause types. In Kazuha Watanabe & Robert B. Young (eds.) *Proceedings of SALT 14*. Ithaca: CLC, pp. 235–252.

Pratt, Mary Louise. 1986. Ideology and speech-act theory. *Poetics Today* 7(1): 59–72.

Recanati, François. 2004a. Pragmatics and semantics. In Laurence R. Horn & Gregory Ward (eds.) *The Handbook of Pragmatics*. Oxford: Blackwell, pp. 442–462.

Recanati, François. 2004b. *Literal Meaning*. Cambridge: Cambridge University Press.

van Rees, M. Agnes. 1992. The adequacy of speech act theory for explaining conversational phenomena: A response to some conversation analytical critics. *Journal of Pragmatics* 17(1): 31–47.

Ross, John R. 1970. On declarative sentences. In Roderick A. Jacobs & Peter S. Rosenbaum (eds.) *Readings in English Transformational Grammar*. Waltham: Ginn, pp. 222–272.

Ruytenbeek, Nicolas, Ekaterina Ostashchenko & Mikhail Kissine. 2017. Indirect request processing, sentence types and illocutionary forces. *Journal of Pragmatics* 119: 46–62.

Sacks, Harvey, Emanuel A. Schegloff & Gail Jefferson. 1974. A simplest systematics for the organisation of turn-taking in conversation. *Language* 50(4): 696–735.

Sadock, Jerrold. 1974. *Toward a Linguistic Theory of Speech Acts*. New York: Academic Press.

Sadock, Jerrold. 2004. Speech acts. In Laurence R. Horn & Gregory Ward (eds.) *The Handbook of Pragmatics*. Oxford: Blackwell, pp. 53–73.

Saul, Jennifer. 2018. Dogwhistles, political manipulation, and philosophy of language. In Daniel Fogal, Daniel W. Harris & Matt Moss (eds.) *New Work on Speech Acts*. Oxford: Oxford University Press, pp. 360–383.

Sbisà, Marina. 1992. Speech acts, effects and responses. In John R. Searle, Herman Parrett & Jef Verschueren (eds.) *(On) Searle on Conversation*. Amsterdam: John Benjamins, pp. 101–111.

Sbisà, Marina. 2007. How to read Austin. *Pragmatics* 17(3): 461–473.

Sbisà, Marina. 2009. Uptake and conventionality in illocution. *Lodz Papers in Pragmatics* 5(1): 33–52.

Sbisà, Marina. 2012. Austin on meaning and use. *Lodz Papers in Pragmatics* 8(1): 5–16.

Sbisà, Marina. 2022. Speech act theory. In Jef Verschueren & Jan-Ola Östman (eds.) *Handbook of Pragmatics*, 2nd ed. Amsterdam: John Benjamins, pp. 1303–1317.

Sbisà, Marina. 2024. *Austinian Themes: Illocution, Action, Knowledge, Truth, and Philosophy*. Oxford: Oxford University Press.

Schegloff, Emanuel A. 1979. Identification and recognition in telephone conversation openings. In George Psathas (ed.) *Everyday Language: Studies in Ethnomethodology*. New York: Irvington, pp. 23–78.

Schneider, Klaus P. & Anne Barron (eds.). 2008. *Variational Pragmatics: A Focus on Regional Varieties in Pluricentric Languages*. Amsterdam: John Benjamins.

Searle, John R. 1968. Austin on locutionary and illocutionary acts. *The Philosophical Review* 77(4): 405–424.

Searle, John R. 1969. *Speech Acts: An Essay in the Philosophy of Language*. Cambridge: Cambridge University Press.

Searle, John R. 1975a. A taxonomy of speech acts. In Keith Gunderson (ed.) *Language, Mind, and Knowledge: Minnesota Studies in the Philosophy of Science*. Minneapolis: University of Minnesota Press, pp. 344–369.

Searle, John R. 1975b. Indirect speech acts. In Peter Cole & Jerry L. Morgan (eds.) *Syntax and Semantics, Vol. 3: Speech Acts*. New York: Academic Press, pp. 59–82.

Searle, John R. 1980. The background of meaning. In John R. Searle, Ferenc Kiefer & Manfred Bierwisch (eds.) *Speech Act Theory and Pragmatics*. Dordrecht: Reidel, pp. 221–232.

Searle, John R. 1983. *Intentionality: An Essay in the Philosophy of Mind*. Cambridge: Cambridge University Press.

Searle, John R. & Daniel Vanderveken. 1985. *Foundations of Illocutionary Logic*. Cambridge: Cambridge University Press.

Sinclair, Alasdair. 1976. *The Sociolinguistic Significance of the Form of Requests in Service Encounters: An Empirical Investigation*. Unpublished PhD thesis: University of Cambridge.

Sperber, Dan & Deirdre Wilson. 1995. *Relevance: Communication and Cognition*, 2nd ed. Oxford: Blackwell.

Sperber, Dan & Deirdre Wilson. 2015. Beyond speaker's meaning. *Croatian Journal of Philosophy* 15: 117–149.

Strawson, Peter F. 1964. Intention and convention in speech acts. *The Philosophical Review* 73(4): 439–460.

Tarski, Alfred. 1944. The semantic conception of truth and the foundations of semantics. *Philosophy and Phenomenological Research* 4(3): 341–376.

Verschueren, Jef. 1987. *Pragmatics as a Theory of Linguistic Adaptation (IPrA Working Document 1)*. Antwerp: International Pragmatics Association

Verschueren, Jef. 2022. The pragmatic perspective. In Jef Verschueren & Jan-Ola Östman (eds.) *Handbook of Pragmatics: Manual*, 2nd ed. Amsterdam: John Benjamins, pp. 1–26.

Weigand, Edda. 1996. The state of the art in speech act theory. *Pragmatics & Cognition* 4(2): 367–406.

Wierzbicka, Anna. 1985. Different cultures, different languages, different speech acts: Polish vs. English. *Journal of Pragmatics* 9(2–3): 145–178.

Wilson, Deirdre & Dan Sperber. 1988. Mood and the analysis of non-declarative sentences. In Jonathan Dancy, Julius Matthew Emil Moravcsik & Christopher Charles Whiston Taylor (eds.) *Human Agency: Language, Duty and Value*. Stanford: Stanford University Press, pp. 77–101.

Wilson, Deirdre & Dan Sperber. 1993. Linguistic form and relevance. *Lingua* 90(1–2): 1–25.

Wilson, Deirdre & Dan Sperber. 2004. Relevance theory. In Laurence R. Horn & Gregory Ward (eds.) *The Handbook of Pragmatics*. Oxford: Blackwell, pp. 607–632.

Wiltschko, Martina. 2021. *The Grammar of Interactional Language*. Cambridge: Cambridge University Press.

Witek, Maciej. 2015. An interactional account of illocutionary practice. *Language Sciences* 47(A): 43–55.

Acknowledgements

I am grateful to the series editors, Jonathan Culpeper and Michael Haugh, for their kind invitation, sound editorial advice and considerable patience, as well as to two anonymous reviewers for their encouragement and truly insightful and constructive feedback. Needless to say, any errors or omissions remain my own. I also need to thank the University of Malta for granting me with sabbatical leave, which enabled me to focus on this work.

This Element is dedicated to my parents, Giorgos and Ritsa, for their unwavering support through the years.

Cambridge Elements

Pragmatics

Jonathan Culpeper
Lancaster University, UK

Jonathan Culpeper is Professor of English Language and Linguistics in the Department of Linguistics and English Language at Lancaster University, UK. A former co-editor-in-chief of the *Journal of Pragmatics* (2009–14), with research spanning multiple areas within pragmatics, his major publications include: Impoliteness: *Using Language to Cause Offence* (2011, CUP) and *Pragmatics and the English Language* (2014, Palgrave; with Michael Haugh).

Michael Haugh
University of Queensland, Australia

Michael Haugh is Professor of Linguistics and Applied Linguistics in the School of Languages and Cultures at the University of Queensland, Australia. A former co-editor-in-chief of the *Journal of Pragmatics* (2015–2020), with research spanning multiple areas within pragmatics, his major publications include: *Understanding Politeness* (2013, CUP; with Dániel Kádár), *Pragmatics and the English Language* (2014, Palgrave; with Jonathan Culpeper), and *Im/politeness Implicatures* (2015, Mouton de Gruyter).

Advisory Board

Anne Baron *Leuphana University of Lüneburg, German*
Betty Birner *Northern Illinois University, USA*
Lucien Brown *Monash University, Australia*
Billy Clark *Northumbria University, UK*
Chris Cummins *University of Edinburgh, UK*
Pilar Garcés-Conejos Blitvich *University of North Carolina at Charlotte, USA*
Andreas Jucker *University of Zurich, Switzerland*
Zohar Kampf *Hebrew University of Jerusalem, Israel*
Miriam A. Locher *Universität Basel*
Yoshiko Matsumoto *Stanford University, USA*
Marina Terkourafi *Leiden University, The Netherlands*
Chaoqun Xie *Zhejiang International Studies University*

About the Series

The Cambridge Elements in Pragmatics series showcases dynamic and high-quality original, concise and accessible scholarly works. Written for a broad pragmatics readership it encourages dialogue across different perspectives on language use. It is a forum for cutting-edge work in pragmatics: consolidating theory (especially through cross-fertilization), leading the development of new methods, and advancing innovative topics in pragmatics.

Cambridge Elements

Pragmatics

Elements in the Series

Positive Social Acts: A Metapragmatic Exploration of the Brighter and Darker Sides of Sociability
Roni Danziger

Pragmatics in Translation: Mediality, Participation and Relational Work
Daria Dayter, Miriam A. Locher and Thomas C. Messerli

Corpus Pragmatics
Daniela Landert, Daria Dayter, Thomas C. Messerli and Miriam A. Locher

Fiction and Pragmatics
Miriam A. Locher, Andreas H. Jucker, Daniela Landert and Thomas C. Messerli

Pragmatics, (Im)Politeness, and Intergroup Communication: A Multilayered, Discursive Analysis of Cancel Culture
Pilar G. Blitvich

Pragmatics, Utterance Meaning, and Representational Gesture
Jack Wilson

Leveraging Relations in Diaspora: Occupational Recommendations among Latin Americans in London
Rosina Márquez Reiter

The Dark Matter of Pragmatics: Known Unknowns
Stephen C. Levinson

Pragmatic Inference: Misunderstandings, Accountability, Deniability
Chi-Hé Elder

Speech Acts: Discursive, Multimodal, Diachronic
Andreas H. Jucker

Pragmatics in the Health Sciences
Maria Garraffa and Greta Mazzaggio

Speech Act Theory: Between Narrow and Broad Pragmatics
Stavros Assimakopoulos

A full series listing is available at: www.cambridge.org/EIPR

For EU product safety concerns, contact us at Calle de José Abascal, 56–1°, 28003 Madrid, Spain or eugpsr@cambridge.org.

www.ingramcontent.com/pod-product-compliance
Lightning Source LLC
LaVergne TN
LVHW011855060526
838200LV00054B/4351